W9-BWE-949

SOCIAL CHANGE
IN AMERICA

*the text of this book is printed
on 100% recycled paper*

SOCIAL CHANGE
IN AMERICA:
THE TWENTIETH CENTURY

THOMAS C. COCHRAN

HARPER ❦ TORCHBOOKS
Harper & Row, Publishers
New York, Evanston, San Francisco, London

301.29
C663a

72-194969

PREFACE

The eight lectures that are the basis of this book were given in the autumn of 1970 (under the joint sponsorship of Raymond Carr, Warden of St Antony's, and Peter Mathias, Chichele Professor of Economic History) while I was a visiting fellow at St Antony's College, Oxford.

In this slightly expanded form I attempt two things: first, to argue for acceptance by historians of a behavioural science approach to social change, and second, to apply such an approach to an interpretation of the history of the United States in the twentieth century. It is not necessary to acquire a detailed understanding of the behavioural paradigm explained in Chapter I in order to understand subsequent interpretive chapters. On the few occasions when a term is employed in a way not usual in everyday speech an explanatory footnote has been added. Documentation is deliberately variable, and while the source of all quotations is given, information taken from well-known material, particularly the censuses, is not footnoted, whereas that from sources less used by historians is.

From one standpoint the resulting interpretation is merely well-accepted institutional history. The difference lies in more emphasis on changes in the socially conditioned habits of behaviour that form institutions than is common to historical accounts concerned with politics, prominent men and arresting events. Applied to twentieth-century America, a social institutional approach treats government as a device for reflecting more basic changes through new political policy. Therefore there is no single chapter on change in political institutions, but rather the inclusion of the government dimension in discussing relevant types of social change. Political change is not necessarily a dependent variable;

in some revolutions it has been a generating force; but to treat the two major disruptive events of this period in the United States, that is the Great Depression and World War II, as the results of antecedent political change distorts the evidence. While government was far from static, its much greater scope of activity in 1970, as compared with 1900, was the gradual result of nearly continuous social pressures, which in a brief survey should be the chief focus of attention.

My colleagues at St Antony's and senior fellows from other colleges who attended the lectures were helpful and provocative in discussions. In addition I want to thank Murray G. Murphey and the late David M. Potter for comments on the theoretical pattern, and Stanley Bailis and Arthur P. Dudden for reading and criticizing the manuscript as a whole.

March 1971   THOMAS C. COCHRAN

CONTENTS

CHAPTER I

A SYSTEMATIC APPROACH
TO CHANGE[1]

Approaches to history are matters of taste and purpose. Some prefer coherent narrative in which the events are selected by use of an unspecified, or perhaps even unconscious, scale of values; others prefer discussion of long-term trends, often with efforts at measurement; and a few try to use the record of past experience to reveal some uniform mechanisms of social change.

While still engaging the interest of only a small minority of historians, this last approach is gaining in popularity, particularly among younger scholars, in the United States. One reason is that the accumulation of thousands of new doctoral theses is overwhelming historians with tolerably accurate secondary material. It is logical for some part of the profession, therefore, to detach itself from the discovery of new facts in order to try to find the larger meanings or utility of this vast collection of monographs and articles in both history and the allied social disciplines.

This course has as obvious corollaries the substitution of analysis for narative, of scope for extensive factual detail, and of the rhetoric of science for that of drama. Since drama is more emotionally moving than science, and narration more exciting than generalization, these substitutions inevitably remove analytical history from the field of popular literature. Yet, to maintain its place in the culture of the present stage of industrialism, it seems

[1] Parts of this chapter have appeared in the *Proceedings of the American Philosophical Society* and are reprinted with permission.

that history must prove that it has some analytical utility. It must move beyond the traditional and undefined justification of 'increased understanding' toward forming a basis for, at least, limited forecasting of the range of social probabilities. If the reader of this book, however, is interested in the general interpretation of what happened in the United States in the twentieth century, rather than in a particular theoretical ordering, he may skip this introductory discussion and still understand the ensuing chapters.

To treat history as a social or analytical science (Charles A. Beard called it a humanistic science), it is necessary to examine some of the conceptual aids to systematic historical understanding offered by the other social disciplines. In employing what is often called a 'social science approach to history', however, one should keep the limitations of all social science method clearly in view. It is said of Chancellor Bismarck presiding in council that after his staff had scoffed at certain factors which they termed 'imponderables', that he reached his decision: 'Gentlemen, the imponderables have it.' The social sciences cannot weigh the unweighables, but they can provide patterns for interrelating some of them that appear to be of value in organizing both current and historical data.[1]

Obviously, the basic purpose of useful history is the explanation of social change. If social structure or cultural patterns were unchanged by great men or events, the latter would have little but the mythological interest they evoke in more static primitive societies. The problem, therefore, is to relate men and events, human decisions and their results, to some reasonably uniform elements in social change.

At present no discipline offers a simple but comprehensive system for doing this. Economic theory has precise methods for forecasting change when the people acting are motivated by com-

[1] For general discussion see Amitai and Eva Etzioni, eds., *Social Change: Sources, Patterns and Consequences*, New York: Basic Books, 1964; Wilbert E. Moore, *Social Change*, Englewood Cliffs, N.J.: Prentice-Hall, 1964; and Werner J. Cahnman and Alvin Boskoff, eds., *Sociology and History: Theory and Research*, New York: Free Press, 1964; London: Collier-Macmillan, 1964. I am also indebted to the discussion by Stanley Bailis in a manuscript thesis, 'The Development and Significance of "Role—Modification Directives" under Rapid Socio-Cultural Change', University of Pennsylvania, 1971.

petition for direct monetary or material returns, and outside, or exogenous, factors do not intrude on the market. Such situations cannot, of course, exist in the real world over any considerable period of time. As T. W. Hutchinson notes, the major expositions of economic theory by such men as Adam Smith, J. S. Mill, Karl Marx, or John Maynard Keynes make social and political assumptions of key importance.[1]

Psychological theory has established a number of apparently valid propositions regarding change involving stimulus, response, and learning, but generally in an isolated or laboratory setting. Hence as guides to social change these concepts share the same weakness as those of the economists.

Anthropologists and sociologists, particularly the latter, have written a great deal about social change, but their theoretical approach to the process itself seems hampered by over-emphasis on the durability of social structure, theories of equilibrium and other essentially static concepts. They tend, that is, to emphasize continuing social relations more than continuous change. Sociologist Wilbert E. Moore writes: 'If the economist's model [of society] tends to be the prize fight, the sociologists' model tends to be the quilting bee.'[2]

The great figures in the literature of change such as Karl Marx, Max Weber, Ferdinand Toennies, Oswald Spengler, or Arnold Toynbee have theorized about great changes from one type of society or civilization to another. In contrast, most behavioural or economic theorists are prone to assume a state of social equilibrium unless some particular force exerts a disruptive influence. Hence they are inclined to talk of 'a change' rather than of the process of change.

In general, historians who have always to deal with social change have, on a working level, eschewed broad hypostheses. Therefore, the social sciences and history collectively are without a comprehensive but reasonably simple categorizing system or

[1] 'Economic Though [sic] and Policy: Generalizations and Ambiguities', *International Congress of Economic History*, Moscow: Nayka, 1970, p. 14.
[2] 'Motivated Aspects of Development', in Etzionis, *op. cit.*, p. 293.

paradigm for dealing with the almost infinite variety of forces involved in continuous social change. For the other social scientists a system explaining long-term change would aid in prediction, for the historian post-diction, or understanding of the past, and in the final analysis the two processes are essentially the same.

The concept of continuous change should not be used to sweep aside the static or, if you like, equilibrating effect of strongly entrenched social institutions. By the usual definitions, institutions involve not only expectations of normally repetitive social conduct, but usually material and formally defined aspects, often imbedded in masonry and laws, as with the church and marriage. Hence, institutions may both inhibit perceptions that would lead to change and offer strong physical resistance to the attrition of institutionally vested interests.

Moving toward a paradigm for continuous change, the possibility for an acceptable system lies in the fact that all of the basic forces—intellectual, institutional, technological, or demographic—operate socially by altering the actions of individuals, and that the behavioural sciences, at least, all use role theory to describe personal activity.[1]

To gain consensus, therefore, it seems best to focus on role-playing as the central process involved in social change, and to relate the other elements to it in a systematic way. The system suggested here has developed over many years, not primarily from theoretical speculation or deduction, but from meeting the need to organize and find meaning in historical data.

To state the paradigm in the simplest terms, people are expected to behave in the various jobs or statuses they occupy in ways that conform to the norms of that society.[2] Each such anticipated pattern of behaviour is a social role. Both normal playing of the role or any change in it will depend on the personality of the player or actor, his motivation for undertaking the role, the resources in knowledge generally available for carrying

[1] See Bruce J. Biddle and Edwin J. Thomas, eds, *Role Theory: Concepts and Research*, New York and Chichester, Sussex: John Wiley, 1966.

[2] Norms are rules of right behaviour for performing specific functions. Values are general attitudes regarding what is right.

out the functions of the role, the reinforcing or retarding effect of social institutions and the pressures upon the player from other people involved in the action.[1] His influence on social change will depend on his innovations affecting institutions, and this, in turn, will depend on his personal status, the type of role and the appeal of the new idea or action.

Many social scientists will probably object that role theory deals only with certain aspects of the problems of change, and that in general it is too much concerned with process or mechanism and not enough with overall structural relationships. But change, after all, is a process, not a structure, and unless there is an initial focus on such a universal behavioural process, analysis tends to become lost in complex structural relations. Role is the key point in the interaction between personality, and its social context, the point at which individuals or groups shape and are shaped by their environment, in other words, roles constitute a form of social structure.[2] Novel role performances, therefore, underlie structural change.

In terms of the paradigm, conventional economic theory, for example, assumes that actors are motivated to play economic roles so as to maximize financial or other satisfactions, on the basis of resources of knowledge freely available and entirely adequate to the aims of the role, and that social institutions and other outside pressures remain stable (the *ceteris paribus* assumption). But in real life none of these conditions can be relied upon. As Herbert A. Simon writes in *Surveys of Economic Theory*, it can be contended 'that the real world is so complicated that the theory of utility maximization has little reference to real choices', and that the actor's 'perceived world is fantastically different from the "real" world'.[3]

---

[1] For an early but extensive discussion of social roles see Leland H. Jenks, 'The Role Structure of Entrepreneurial Personality,' in *Change and the Entrepreneur*, Research Center in Entrepreneurial History, Harvard University, Cambridge, Mass.: Harvard University Press, 1949, pp. 108–52.

[2] Herbert A. Simon, 'Theories of Decision-Making in Economic and Behavioral Sciences', in *Surveys of Economic Theory*, prepared for the American Economic Association and the Royal Economic Society, New York: St Martin's Press, 1967, Vol. 3, pp. 6–7.

[3] See Bailis, *op. cit.*, Ch. I.

Subsequent chapters will interpret change in the United States in the twentieth century in relation to the assumptions of the paradigm, but meanwhile it may be helpful to gain familiarity with the role system by briefly exemplifying its use. Such illustration will suggest how it may help, at least, to systematize some of the complications and limitations that historians or other scholars have to deal with in empirical research. In general, while the American data show values and situations favourable to change and development, they also suggest factors inimical to change. Furthermore, in contrast to so much of the theorizing about change that is in terms of the gross shifts from what are termed 'traditional' to 'modern' societies, North American illustrations show the subtler changes that take place in a society which from its beginnings could, by the standards of its day, be called 'modern'.

Since all the elements of the system are interconnected in an 'organic' way there is no logical order of presentation. I will start first with the personality of the actor which is the hardest category to determine from historical evidence.[1] By most psychologists, the adult is assumed to have a roughly ascertainable 'character' resulting from the usual forces conditioning childhood and youth in the particular society, but this may vary because of imperfect socialization, arising from a number of causes such as education in a dissident sect or migration from another culture. This conditioned character leads the actor to want to play a role in a way satisfactory to some real or symbolic person who is called his reference group, an entity frequently unavailable from historical evidence, as well as to satisfy his subconscious motivations. Hence to learn all the different conditioning forces bearing on the youth of society in any generation and the different reference groups and types of perception that they produce is also probably impossible. But where recruitment for a role brings to it people of the same general education, environment and social

[1] For a psychoanalytic discussion of personality, not contradictory to what follows here, see Erich Fromm, *Man for Himself*, Greenwich, Conn.: Fawcett, 1947 (pp. 58–69), London, Routledge, 1945.

status, 'character' becomes sufficiently uniform to be a hypothetically usable factor.

Take, for example, the successful corporate executive of the late nineteenth century. Studies indicate that normally (or modally) he was reared in a religiously devout family whose head was in business in a town or city, and educated in a conventional secondary school. Perhaps a third or more such men attended college.[1] These measurable common elements plus indirect written evidence regarding middle-class child-rearing practices provide a basis for generalizations regarding modal character.

But character is only one of the two major elements in most of the present conceptions of personality. The other, perception or 'cognition' of the environment is associated with values and attitudes of the culture as well as the particular conditioning (or socialization) of the actor. Since men with similar learning, experience, and desires will tend to see the same aspects of their environment, some generalizations are possible regarding uniformities in this element. Hence, 'personality', which depends on the interplay of inward character and perception of the outward situation, is a variable subject to some limitations or assumptions as to modes.

The historian, in practice, usually comes to the analysis of personality from the opposite direction. From accumulating evidence he finds uniformities in response to certain situations, and these suggest positive and negative aspects of perception and other characters of a modal personality. Among people of the United States one can historically document characteristics such as high motivation for success, optimism, and emphasis on activity as a virtue in itself. With their attention focused on material expansion, Americans, for example, perceived economic opportunities which would have gone unnoticed in a more static, traditionally oriented society.

This general or shared knowledge determines whether, on the

[1] See William Miller, ed., *Men in Business*, Cambridge, Mass: Harvard University Press, 1953 (pp. 29, 220), London: Harper & Row; Thomas C. Cochran, *Railroad Leaders: The Business Mind in Action, 1845–1890*, Cambridge, Mass.: Harvard University Press, 1953, p. 220.

basis of the normal perception of the situation, a man wants to occupy the status to which an anticipated role is attached. As societies become more developed economically and the basic need for self-support plays a smaller part, such decisions seem increasingly influenced by social or cultural factors. Anthropologist Evon Z. Vogt has written: 'The importance of value orientation in shaping the direction of change is proportional to the economic and technological control as society has achieved.'[1] In apparent contrast Clark Kerr and associates, in *Industrialism and Industrial Man*, claim that cultural differences are more important at the beginning of industrialization than in the later stages.[2] But the Kerr team are talking of the shift from agrarian to industrial society, and Vogt about later increases in the level of economic output.

While a man's decision will depend, in large part, on the rewards to be hoped for from occupying a position in relation to the attractiveness of the alternatives, the nature of what is appealing as a reward will reflect the hierarchy of values and the institutional structure of the particular culture. 'Rewards' may not be measured in economic values, and their effectiveness or lack of effectiveness will depend on both the culture and the social class from which the actors are recruited.

In many less industrialized societies, for example, maximum profit may not be the ultimate goal of a business venture. The entrepreneur's aim may be social prestige, maintenance of his position as head of the family through providing employment for his relatives, or securing just enough money to take up some more desired type of life. In modern Europe and in present-day United States it has often been difficult to keep successful entrepreneurial families devoted to business rather than to more pleasant or satisfying but less financially remunerative activities. Of every role-player it has to be asked, not only how high is his motivation for achievement, and how good his prospects for success, but also what are the true reasons for undertaking the

---

[1] *American Anthropologist*, 61 (Feb. 1960), 266.
[2] London: Oxford University Press, 1964.

role. Talcott Parsons and Edward A. Shills contend that for a social system to function 'roles should provide a minimum of essential gratification'.[1] This suggests a further hypothesis, that roles may be played best along the lines that give the actor the most satisfaction, which may be a crucial element of difference in the playing of the same role in various cultures.

The resources in knowledge available to the actor for executing the functions of the role depend initially upon his perception of the situation, which, in turn, arises from his share in the level and type of learning in the particular culture. This is, of course, an immense category, susceptible to being broken down into sub-divisions such as factual knowledge and its interpretation, beliefs and their expression in systems of thought, customary attitudes and the types of insights they emphasize or preclude, as well as the means of disseminating information to those who can use it. Historians dealing with changes in and transfers of ideas, for example, may use explanatory sub-hypotheses some of which will be discussed later. For the present overall paradigm, social learning at a particular time and place is a 'given' or parameter, but the extent to which any one man shares in this learning depends not only on his personality and ability but on the role he is playing, his social class, and the type of education in the society as well as on the channels for flows of information.

In considering this aspect of role-performance some widely accepted propositions are useful. One advanced by both psychologists and anthropologists is that people see only what they have been conditioned to see, or as Goethe put it: 'We see only what we know.' Responses will, therefore, lie within the bounds of the range and type of imagination fostered by the social learning. The demands of the particular role being played may enable the actor to perceive all that he is familiar with in the directions emphasized by the role, while elements not needed for the anticipated performance of the role will be overlooked, even if they are part of the generally shared social learning. As Professor Simon says: 'The sins of omission in perception are more impor-

---

[1] 'The Content of Roles', in Biddle and Thomas, *op. cit.*, p. 239.

tant than the sins of commission.'[1] This seeing with blinkers, or over-selectivity, was called by Thorstin Veblen 'trained incapacity'. It is so familiar to every scholar in his own work that it scarcely needs illustration. Business executives, brilliant in performing the major functions of their role, have often been quite inept in perceiving unwanted related problems, such as those connected with labour relations, even though the necessary knowledge was widely shared in the culture.

Another way of saying this is that interpretation of a situation by the actor is likely to be based on projection of the orientation inculcated by his personal conditioning and the normal social role, rather than by recognition of the external realities. The emphasis on national honour and military force in the role of the chief of state, for example, often blinds such actors to cheaper and more generally satisfactory alternatives.

Even in rapidly changing societies the need for reliable roles inculcates negative attitudes that block out realities not consistent with the orientations of the culture. Acceptance of this hypothesis is a considerable aid in understanding change through innovation. While the combinations and permutations of known elements in any advanced culture are for practical purposes infinite and, therefore, ideas or inventions inconceivable in advance emerge from time to time, their degree of acceptance presumably follows existing patterns of the culture.

Several studies of the writing of a number of similarly placed individuals have indicated the availability, under certain conditions at least, of the material necessary to define the limits of the normal or model range of imaginative construction, and, therefore, to understand the reason for apparently novel reactions in some historical situations.[2] Crude rank orders may even be set up for the probability of certain types of response on the basis of geographic area and types of educational and occupational conditioning.

[1] *Op. cit.*, p. 19.
[2] See Cochran, *Railroad Leaders*, pp. 218–20; *The Puerto Rican Businessman: A Study in Cultural Change*, Philadelphia: University of Pennsylvania Press, 1959, pp. 117–32; and Cochran and Reuben E. Reina, *Entrepreneurship in Argentine Culture: Torcuato Di Tella and S.I.A.M.*, Philadelphia: University of Pennsylvania Press, 1962, pp. 250–70.

Without regard, however, to such fine distinctions, some general types of cases seem important for innovation. One is where the actor has learned the routine ways of the local culture imperfectly, or, as the psychologists would say, has acquired deviant learning-sets. This may result either from being brought up outside the culture or from an eccentric conditioning or socialization. Both are aspects of the same process. A man like William James, brought up in Europe as an aristocrat and educated in European schools, was essentially being conditioned outside American culture. Such men have beliefs or attitudes that may be out of tune with certain roles they are expected to play, and this sets up what Leon Festinger has called 'dissonance'.[1] Conversely it can result from the essential needs of roles changing faster than general beliefs.

The more common aspect of imperfect socialization in American history, however, was that of migrants either between Europe and America, where the imperfections in understanding and differences in emotional responses might be great, or between regions in the United States, where the differences might be subtle. But in either case, the in-migrant, probably a young adult, might innovate in the very process of adjustment.[2] The other frequent cause for innovation is extreme specialization, in both education and imagination, on limited aspects of the social learning, illustrated by men like Edison or Ford. This is equivalent to saying that inventions and innovations usually arise from men who bring deviant knowledge to a role or unusual emotional fixation on certain processes.[3]

The type of social learning in a nation is, of course, the product of a wide range of factors such as economic opportunity, historical traditions, and social and political systems. Socioeconomic factors such as the relations between land, labour, capital, and technology, for example, are in all nations reflected

---

[1] Biddle and Thomas, *op. cit.*, p. 328.
[2] H. G. Barnett, *Innovation: The Basis of Cultural Change*, New York: McGraw-Hill, 1953, pp. 87–90.
[3] See Everett M. Rogers, *Diffusion of Innovations*, New York: Free Press, 1962, *passim*, including an extensive bibliography.

in prevailing attitudes or cultural biases that strongly affect role-playing decisions. In the United States these relations made the market the ultimate sanction in most decisions. In this broad social context, however, a market is not a mechanism where supply is acted upon demand and price results automatically, but rather a meeting of human decision-makers each with an inner conception or bias regarding the probable course of the situation. In the continental United States optimism regarding future demand was a prevailing bias, leading to a continuous trend toward over-commitment; whereas in Puerto Rico pessimism, stemming from the limited possibilities of local markets, produced a bias toward inertia and avoidance of risks. Similarly, major systems of thought, such as the Christian religion, dominate both perception and intellectual attitudes, producing general biases or incapacities in the playing of roles.

Turning from the actor's perception of the situation in terms of his knowledge and values to another major category of the paradigm, the external resources available for achieving the desired ends, one moves into the area of readily ascertainable factual data. There is, for example, the support that the institutional structure of the society gives both to recruitment to and expectations of success in a given role. Assumed stability in the institutions of government, for example, was such a support in the United States. Statements regarding expectations in various roles are often available in correspondence, or can be reconstructed in the light of history. Such analyses can lead to rank orders of institutional elements, such as the family, religion or the law, in the facilitating or hindering the carrying out of a particular function.

The last of the major categories of influence bearing upon the actor, or decision-maker, consists of the pressures of individuals or groups generally reflecting existing social institutions, such as the parishioners of a Protestant minister, or the board of directors of a corporate executive—people able effectively to sanction the playing of the role. Robert Merton and other sociologists have called these groups role-sets. Together with the roles they

comprise the operating mechanisms of social structure. The role-
-sets determine, for example, what one must learn to be conven-
tionally socialized. There will normally be several such groups
associated with a role, and they may have different desires as to
how the role should be played. While they vary in their power to
enforce their wishes, the actor normally tries to live up to the
expectations of as many as possible of these groups and resorts
to strategies to counterbalance or avoid adverse sanctions.[1]

Sometimes, as in demographic change, cause and effect may
operate very slowly. As a city grows larger, for example, roles
reach points where they are so dysfunctional that change is
necessary, but just when this point comes in a given type of role
during such 'institutional drift' may vary from case to case. In
addition, some basic alterations in either physical or intellectual
environment may set up ambiguous or opposing reactions in
role-sets and on role-players, as in the early stages of the conflict
between science and religion, which produced both inconsistent
behaviour and confused sanctions.

Normally, role-sets and role-players are guided in their expectations by accepted social institutions and these stem, in turn,
from uniform role performances over considerable time periods,
gradually modified by the pressures of physical change and new
ideas. Even though the two elements are inextricably related, since
institutions are, by definition, relatively fixed and known forms of
behaviour, individual role-playing is the more dynamic element
in change. A single successful innovation may permanently
change a social role, while existing institutions tend to be a counter
force. Yet not all changes in role are initiated by innovation or
deviation from the norms by only a single individual. In fact,
some psychologists have found people approached in groups more
susceptible to change than when approached individually.
Changing climates of opinion such as from faith to scepticism,
optimism to pessimism or some passing fashion affect both the
actor and his role-set and may strongly influence decisions. In a

---

[1] Robert K. Merton, 'Instability and Articulation in the Role Set', in Biddle and
Thomas, *op. cit.*, p. 282.

period of rapid change new sanctions introduced by the role-sets as groups will be an important force.

Efforts to avoid tensions or adjust to *zeitgeists* may be in themselves a source of change, but in addition a developing society presents novel situations where the expectations of the role-set are relatively undefined, leaving the social role loosely structured. Since in such situations the role-player also lacks a precise conception how to act, innovation is likely, but, again, it will be culturally conditioned and therefore in part predictable rather than random. As already noted, migration to a new area is a cause of such uncertainties and hence of innovation.[1]

The preceding discussion has been chiefly concerned with assumptions arising from empirical evidence on the effect of cultural and physical continuities and changes on role-playing. Child socialization, systems of values, and social learning have been related to the role-player's perception of the situation and how he is likely to react. Some aspects of socialization and migration have been seen as particularly likely to cause innovation in roles.

The most complex and difficult problem of the paradigm is the interrelationship between changes in role-playing and general social change. If this interaction were not so varied and hard to estimate, there would by now be a comprehensive and well-accepted social science theory of change. But, here again, an orderly arrangement of factors based on role theory can be a step toward further scientific progress. Talcott Parsons affirms the fact that, to cause social change, a deviation in role must be incorporated at the next higher or more generalized level of social structure which, in the present paradigm, means in a controlling part of the role-set.[2]

If this group, whose views of the role has been changed, persuades or compels similar role-sets to adopt the new idea the change will have been institutionalized. Obviously for a time there will be two views of the role, the old and the new, perhaps

[1] Barnett, *op. cit.*, pp. 87–93.
[2] 'A Functional Theory of Change', in Etzionis, *op. cit.*, p. 95.

in serious conflict, and victory or suppression of the change will depend on the force of the institutional innovators in their personal relations and perhaps in the use of mass media and the power structure. Revolution, for example, may be seen as forceful readjustment in the sanctioning strength of different role-sets.

The many variables involved in this process of the spread of role change include types of change, the degree of acceptance, and the characteristics of the culture. One classification of types is by information, attitudes, and action. Clearly information can spread without in itself involving any change in the structure and operation of society. Multitudes of statements may be believed or disbelieved without producing attendant action. Information such as Marxian philosophy which implies social action may be known but not utilized.

Attitudinal change implies an impact on the inner role directives or values of actors and therefore involves emotional reactions beyond the mere passive acceptance of information. A spread of Marxian philosophy on the attitudinal level might involve initial resistance, conversion, and social commitment. While mass media serve for the spread of information, interpersonal relations (reciprocal role relationships), usually of an intimate type, are generally involved in attitudinal changes.[1]

Change involving action may come either from information (learning of some new process or device) or attitudinal pressure where one is urged, for example, to support a cause with time and money. Even in just putting across information about the new, interpersonal relations, or personal examination of the novel device or process, has been found to be of decisive importance. Twentieth-century American farmers, for instance, generally acted on the basis of demonstrations by county agents rather than on the information in agricultural journals.[2]

The degree of social acceptance of change forms a continuous

[1] Forsten Hägerstrand, 'The Diffusion of Innovations', *International Encyclopaedia of the Social Sciences*, New York: Free Press; Macmillan, 1968, 4, p. 176.

[2] See Herbert F. Lionberger, *Adoption of New Ideas and Practices*, Arnes: Iowa State University Press, 1960.

scale from zero to a hundred percent. In history, a change is usually regarded as established when it commands a majority or becomes an accepted norm or value. But every advanced society lives with many conflicting institutions, norms and values, and holds together as long as certain more dominant ones provide sufficient justification for the *status quo*. Change comes from the continual erosion of dominant systems and the rise of those from the formerly dissident minority. Or, seeing culture as the organization of diversity, there is a change in the weighting of the diverse elements.

The differing characteristics of culture in relation to change are so much the subject of historical writing that they scarcely need exemplification. Each culture has different dimensions of rigidity and fluidity, and these tend to be reinforced over time. It is seldom that innovating jumps are large. An agricultural country, no matter how willing, cannot quickly be turned into an industrial nation by intensive training, capital and machinery. Each major innovation needs useful supporting roles and institutions, or, one might say, blocks with which to build. In the direction in which a culture has been moving these supports will be numerous, and the change will probably be continuous and readily absorbed into many allied institutional roles. The introduction of new forms in art and music in France of the late nineteenth century had its difficulties, but supporting roles were numerous and diverse and the changes won acceptance. In the United States the knowledge of such innovations had small effect because it involved few roles or institutions and occasioned little support or rejection. On the other hand, American culture offered less resistance to new machinery and many practical processes than was the case in Europe, because such change was partly institutionalized or anticipated.

In the same vein, what is 'logically' convincing in one culture may not be so in another, yet each society will accept change on the basis of what they regard as reasonable. Murray G. Murphey sees changes in ideas and resulting institutions as 'a function of the relation between evidential experience and degrees of belief', regardless of whether the change involves science, religion or habitual customs.[1] In 'evidential experience' statements by forceful personalities, operating either face to face or through mass media, carry much weight.

Among the many roles of an advanced industrial society some prescribe actions that are likely to produce change, such as those of city-planners or corporate development directors, and the dynamism and ability to achieve new adjustment in a society will depend greatly on the influence and relative number of such roles. Anthropologist Ward H. Goodenough calls the players of these roles 'agents of change' and sees social change as a function of the interaction of such agents with the institutional forces of continuity or resistance.[2]

Whether or not actors consciously intend to alter their roles in ways conducive to institutional change, there is a virtually unavoidable tension between individual goals and the institutional means for achieving them that generates change. People play the same role or join the same social organizations from highly diverse motivations. Consequently, when new situations arise reactions differ and the organization or institution either readjusts or disintegrates. Furthermore, as roles become increasingly numerous and diversified, their interaction inevitably produces new ideas and attitudes, and both actors and their role-sets become accustomed to change.[3] Such considerations practically ensure change merely from the passage of time.

So far the discussion has emphasized change when, in fact, the interpersonal relations relied on to reinforce novel risk-taking are usually a restraining force. Logically, the people of a culture represent the norms and values of the culture, and thus when the potential innovator confers with others he is most likely to receive conservative advice. It is these intimate interpersonal relations

[1] 'On the Relations Between Science and Religion', *American Quarterly*, XX (Summer 1968) Supplement, p. 294.
[2] *Cooperation in Change: An Anthropological Approach to Community Development*, New York: Wiley, 1963, pp. 19 ff.
[3] See Bailis, *op. cit.*, Ch. III; and also, C. D. W. Goodwin and I. B. Holley, Jr., 'The Transfer of Ideas', *South Atlantic Quarterly*, 67 (Spring 1968).

that preserve group norms, hold the society together, and give cultures their remarkable continuity.[1]

Conversely, mass media probably have their strongest persuasive force where for some reason personal discussion of the issue is absent. On this basis impersonal urban culture should be most open to influence by media. Also, since many people avoid discussing 'controversial subjects', this may permit the subtle penetration of new ideas in a hostile milieu more rapidly than in a slightly favourable one where the ideas would be discussed and dismissed, hence the sudden welling-up of underground revolutionary forces in repressed societies.

The major thrust of diffusion and communication theory, therefore, is to emphasize the importance of intimate interpersonal communication or reciprocal role playing. Yet the historian is seldom able to find records at this level. Necessarily he deals with resulting institutional changes when they have won sufficient acceptance to gain visibility in some type of record. Thus, while not the basic building blocks of social structure, institutions are the easily recognized characteristics of the edifice, those that provide a convenient level for discourse and generalization regarding social situations.

The problems inherent in the discussion of institutional change involve the weaknesses of all scientific knowledge: the questions determine the answers, and the indexes chosen govern the statistics. Granting that cultural biases give rise to questions and types of measurements, in addition well-accepted social science mechanisms, such as those discussed here, are often too generalized to provide adequate 'operational' answers, and one must rely on tacit historical judgement. As Michael Polanyi observes 'we can know more than we can tell', or readily conceptualize.[2] The mind is a more versatile instrument than the artifices we use to aid it. While Loren Eisley warns that complete understanding of 'the wild reality always eludes your grasp', a systematic approach can

[1] Elilu Katz, 'Diffusion: Interpersonal Influence', *International Encyclopaedia of the Social Sciences*, 4, pp. 182–83.

[2] *The Tacit Dimension*, Garden City, N.Y.: Doubleday, 1966, p. 4.

suggest many new questions, answer a few, and better define the remainder.[1]

Systematic analysis of United States history from 1900 to 1970 indicates that most of the major social roles and institutions of the former date had either changed radically or become dysfunctional by the latter. There is little argument among either historians or other social scientists about the basic forces of change during this period, such as the advance of urban-industrialism with important new technology, attendant shifts in population, the rise of science, and the development of the welfare state. The area of interest, and of debate, is in the specific operation of such forces on human behaviour and institutions. The following chapters will concentrate on estimation of the major institutional changes and their interaction as illuminated by the role paradigm.

[1] *The Unexpected Universe*, New York: Harcourt, Brace, 1969, p. 21.

CHAPTER II

THE INNER REVOLUTION

In the nineteenth century England, Western Europe, and the United States began an unplanned investment in social change through supporting research in universities, government agencies and private foundations. The investment gradually earned not only returns in improved health and productive technology but also some unwanted dividends in the form of socially upsetting scientific and social theories that ultimately altered the intellectual climate of the Western World.

The Christian dogmas of two millennia were challenged by ideas regarding the evolution of man, the limitations of his mind and the nature of the physical universe. While as late as 1890, in the United States, an authoritative pronouncement of 'God's will' was still for most men sufficient to justify the demands for conformity which society imposed upon its members, by 1930 for many educated leaders it was not, and the latter had to find new justifications for life and action.

The history of the United States during this interval presents an unusually interesting study in the interaction of all the social and technological change that both created and disturbed a mature industrial society. At the start America presented a unique contrast: technologically, it was practically abreast of the most advanced Western nations and in scale of operations it was about to become the leader; but in some of the intellectual trends that were to dominate change in the twentieth century it was well behind the leaders. Hence the rapid intellectual changes from 1900 to World War II, while ultimately stemming from the vast process of industrialization, seem the most important new social phenomena. During this period the educated élite in the United States caught up with most of the disturbing knowledge of Western Europe and thereafter shared in the harassed search for acceptable new values.

Among Europeans the fifteen hundred-year-old institutions of the agrarian, Judaeo-Christian morality and its culture had been eroded throughout the nineteenth century, whereas in the United States deism and rationalism had been largely overcome by the forces of a militant clerical intellectualism emanating from New England. The authoritarian, Christian, middle-class morality with strict social norms or sanctions, espoused by the controlling political and business élites, met little effective challenge before the late 1880s. An intense religiosity, particularly among the educated upper-middle class, spilled over into business and the professions. Getting ahead with one's own work and duty to God were easily confused, not only by aggressive entrepreneurs like John D. Rockefeller, Sr., but also by physicists like Willard Gibbs, an ordained congregational minister, and by other religiously trained scientists. Churchmen staffed the boards of the private institutions of higher learning, lower education was regarded as valuable primarily for moral indoctrination, and politicians, both conservative and liberal, seldom failed to invoke the deity with a measured frequency.

This diffusion of religious justification had from the early days produced a sense of mission, a belief that well-played roles were advancing God's kingdom. In colonial times it sufficed for the commercial élite of New England to see their province as God's example to Europe and the Americas, the city upon a hill. By the end of the nineteenth century the sense of mission had expanded to spreading His kingdom, as only Anglo-Saxons could, to all the rest of the world.

Since the major sanctions affecting role-playing in the materially expanding American society were in reality based upon utility, or the market, this rationalization in terms of Christian mission and morality produced a nearly continuous state of tension in most actors and in the members of the role-sets that had to sanction the performance.[1] Religion has perhaps always been an uncomfortable justification for privileged members of the élite. Thus the stage was set for men who became familiar with the new learning rapidly to replace the rigid sanctions of religion by the more flexible ones of science.

This may explain the ease with which scientific sanctions were accepted, but not how the ideas on which the changes in sanctions were based spread to social attitudes and institutions. On this problem the psychologist and philosopher William James wrote to his English friend, Graham Wallas, in 1908: 'The power of certain individuals to infect . . . others is to me almost the all in all of social change.[2] Such influential people occur at all social levels and are generally more effective in spreading an innovation or idea by face-to-face discussion than by writing. The agents of change who introduced European scientific learning into the United States were largely academic scholars such as James, Richard T. Ely or John R. Commons—men who personally influenced students and other scholars, while reaching a wider public through their writing in monographs, texts, and books for the general reader.

Until the 1870s American colleges and universities were small, with only a few hundred students even in the largest, and given over to undergraduate training for the ministry, the law, or simply the acquiring of a genteel ability to read Greek and Latin. Starting with Harvard in 1869, graduate programmes on the German model were introduced, and aspiring students with sufficient money took doctors' degrees in Germany. By the 1880s the influx of scholars bringing back European knowledge of the sciences and history began to have a strong effect on American ideas.

Meanwhile, Darwinian evolution, and the assumed social

[1] Footnotes explanatory of theory will be indicated by an asterisk. Institution, sanction, role and role-set will be virtually the only special terms used in the text. Except for the last one, these terms have become part of the common language. Role-set is simpler than its equivalent, 'the groups that define the social role,' or 'those whose expectations the player seeks to satisfy'.

[2] Kenneth McNaught, 'American Progressives and the Great Society', *Journal of American History*, LIII (December 1966), p. 512.

corollaries of his doctrine of the survival of the fittest from competitive struggle, had been widely promulgated by the writings and American visit of Herbert Spencer who, although an Englishman, had much more influence in the United States than in his homeland. A host of journalists and educators, almost unconsciously substituting 'best' for 'fittest' spread Spencer's 'Social Darwinism' in speeches, articles, editorials, and books. Acceptance of the new ideas reduced the pressure of religious sanctions on roles, alleviating both internal conflicts and those imposed by the role-set. Not only were religious sanctions weakened by the repudiation of Genesis, but the strength of justification by science was given to the usually conflicting sanctions of the competitive market. In addition, Darwinism, reinforced by 'scientific' historical analysis, continued to undermine the literal credibility of all revealed religion, and to make doctrinal sanctions steadily weaker in both seminaries and denominational colleges.

The new ideas, emphasizing scepticism and utility, fitted readily into American roles and institutions and generated a faith that scientific knowledge and procedures might soon solve all questions. The 'scientific society' became the goal of journalists, philanthropists, and political reformers, while the principles needed for such a society appeared easy to evolve. The sociologist Daniel Bell sees the success of a social movement as dependent on doing three things: 'Simplify ideas, establish a claim to truth and in the union of the two demand a commitment to action.'[1] In the first decade and a half of the twentieth century a simplified naïve scientism blended with an optimism born of new economic power to help produce what is generally referred to as the period of progressive reform. Illustrating the arrogant optimism of the period, Woodrow Wilson said in 1901: 'No other modern nation has been schooled as we have in big undertakings and mastery of novel difficulties . . . determining its own destiny unguided and

[1] *The End of Ideology*, New York: Free Press, 1960 (p. 396), London: Collier–Macmillan, 1960.

unbidden, moving as it pleases within wide boundaries, using institutions, not dominated by them.'[1]

Much the same currents of intellectual confidence were present in England and the dominions and to a lesser extent on the Continent, and the Western World seemed to be entering an age of higher civilization. But in the older nations the shift in moral sanctions from religion to science had a longer history, and the hope of soon reaching a social utopia was less naïve and compelling. No one wrote 'The promise of English life' as the journalist Herbert Croly did for the United States; no European was inspired to equal the sociologist E. A. Ross's *Sin and Society* as a forecast of a new social morality, and no British economist had the faith of Simon Patton in the revolutionary effects to be expected from 'the economy of abundance'. Professor Patton said in 1905: 'Disease, oppression, irregular work, pressure, old age, and race hatreds characterize the vanishing age of deficit; plenty of food, shelter, capital, security, and mobility of men and goods define the age of surplus in which we act.'[2]

From the longer view of changing roles and institutional sanctions, the most important of the new sciences appears to have been psychology and its offshoot, psychiatry. The principal early carrier of the European, largely Germanic, ideas to the United States was William James, who in almost every respect fits the definition of a role-player likely to innovate in a way productive of social change.

In the egalitarian United States of the late Jacksonian era, James's father, possessing inherited mercantile wealth, found the intellectual milieu confining and uncongenial. Consequently, William, born in 1842, spent most of the formative period of his life in various European schools and cities. At first he was undecided whether to pursue painting or science, and, ultimately choosing the latter, he was torn between medical and psychological theory. From eight years of study at Harvard he received an

[1] Quoted in Merle E. Curti, 'Woodrow Wilson's Concept of Human Nature', *Midwest Journal of Political Science*, I (May 1957), pp. 12–13.
[2] *The New Basis of Civilization*, New York: Macmillan, 1907 and 1921, p. 186.

M.D. degree and took a position in the medical school. After a few years of psychologically slanted lectures he became, more appropriately for that day, a professor of philosophy. Thus James brought together in his personality the effects of migration on new perceptions, a deviant or imperfect learning of the ways of American culture, the introspection produced by ambiguities as to what major role he wanted to play, and the potential for innovation inherent in a change in occupation.

In 1890, James won general acceptance of his ideas by students and teachers on all levels with a book, *The Principles of Psychology*, which synthesized the new science based on laboratory experiments. The scientific findings undermined the traditional view of man as a rational animal and the religious ideas of self-determination through will-power.[1] Going through many editions, this book and other more popular writings of James became the standard works on psychology for highly educated leaders in all walks of life. In fact, most of the ideas in psychology up to 1970, at least, can trace some line of their ancestry back to the brilliant insights of James.

Most citizens, however, even those of the recognized élites, did not read books or even popular articles on academic psychology.[2] The powerful impact of the new psychological idea that man was governed more by unconscious emotions than by reason reached the United States a generation later from the work of the Viennese medical practitioner, Sigmund Freud.

In the early days of the century, Freud's techniques of a psychoanalysis, of curing mental conflicts or traumas by searching long and expensively through a free association of ideas for the cause assumed to be concealed in the subconscious 'id' or admonitory 'super-ego', won fame in parts of Europe and, after 1910, limited recognition in the United States. A number of wartime cures of

[1] Merle E. Curti, *The Growth of American Thought*, New York: Harper & Row, 3rd edn., 1964 (pp. 543–4), London: Harper & Row, 1964.

[2] It is assumed here that Americans of the turn of the century recognized businessmen, lawyers, and politicians as the élites wielding power, while clergymen, various professionals and intellectuals were seen as élites deserving respect, but not as possessors of much social force.

battle fatigue or neuroses gave psychoanalytic techniques a medical sanction by neurologists in the United States medical corps that led to a wave of Freudianism in the 1920s. Prosperous Americans may not have been interested in psychology as an abstract discipline, but they were interested in curing or contemplating their own neuroses, or in learning how to diagnose those of their friends, and in how to bring up their children in ways that would avoid such troubles.

Changes in values are probably most important for changing roles, and Freudianism was an approach to behaviour heavily laden with values that gave the role-player a quite opposite set of internal guides or sanctions to those supplied by the old Protestant morality. Specifically repudiating religion, Freud's model appeared to turn old-fashioned morality upside down: resistance to urges might be psychologically dangerous; indulgence could be beneficial; and, in any case, infantile repression of sexual desires was the cause of most neuroses. This doctrine of indulgence was not what Freud intended, but it is a fair representation of popular belief in his theories, and it fitted well with a decade of prosperity in which higher consumption through instalment buying, freedom of thought and action for women, and self-centred individualism for all were being emphasized as never before.

Reinforcing Freud in his attack on the supremacy of rational consciousness was the academic psychologist John B. Watson of the University of Chicago. Taking off from the experiments of Pavlov in Russia on the conditioned reflex in animals, Watson reached the conclusion that consciousness was an unscientific fiction and all so-called thought and activity depended on conditioning. His book, *Psychology From the Standpoint of a Behaviorist*, published in 1919, attracted wide academic attention and was more easily grasped than Freudianism by the layman. In the middle twenties the United States Children's Bureau incorporated behaviourist views in its child-care manuals.

Perhaps the most important early impact of both psychiatry and the new psychology was on child-rearing practices. Since a very large part of the moralistic, value-laden aspects of the culture and of anticipated role performances depend upon the admonitions and unexpressed attitudes of parents to children, ideas that alter such relations are of basic importance to social change. The Freudian and Watsonian ideas were only the final stage of an increasing introduction of new psychological theories in child-rearing manuals, reinforced by articles in family and women's magazines. In the late nineteenth century the family had an authoritative caste, and parental admonitions were in terms of God's laws, which included all others. The books and articles on child-rearing were generally written by women or clergymen; by the 1920s the authors were chiefly medical men, and the admonitions were in terms of physiology and psychology.[1]

The effect of the new literature, largely confined to the upper income groups, was an emphasis on permissiveness ('let the child learn for itself'), explanation of the need for any disciplinary measures used and avoidance of anger or corporal punishment. The maximum of permissiveness in both home and school was probably reached between 1925 and 1930, but while depression and war arrested the trend, Max Lerner, in the 1950s, still wrote of a 'deference vacuum' and 'child centred anarchy' in the family.

This breakdown of authority, or of the hierarchical principles, in the family was to be paralleled by similar changes in other institutions inherited from the aristocratic agrarian past. The first breakdown of hierarchy had come long since with the introduction of increasingly democratic forms of government in the United States between 1775 and 1840, but other basic institutions had been more resistant to change.[2]

Although European observers had seen signs of deterioration

[1] Geoffrey Steere, 'Changing Values in Child Sterilization: A Study of United States Child-Rearing Literature, 1865–1929', University of Pennsylvania Ph.D. thesis 1954. For a brief account see Thomas C. Cochran, *The Inner Revolution: Essays on History and the Social Sciences*, New York: Torchbooks, 1965; Magnolia, Mass.: Peter Smith, 1969; London: Harper & Row, Ch. I.

[2] Talcott Parsons, and anthropologists such as Florence Kluckholm, see all societies as built up around basic patterns of belief that vary between opposites such as hierarchy in contrast to equality (the 'pattern variables'), and to alter any of these is significantly to change the foundations of the culture or societal order.

of the hierarchical principle in American family structure throughout the nineteenth century, the authority of parents, reinforced by law, remained strong, particularly among families in less-educated, lower-income groups. But scholars question whether even in the minority of families that adopted more permissiveness or democratic decision-making in the 1920s the parents succeeded in avoiding the transference of many 'outworn' or authoritarian moral and social customs. Mothers and fathers were the product of their own upbringing, and tones of voice, facial expressions, and language, inherited from an earlier age, perhaps had more effect on the child than did the consciously applied precepts of writers on child-rearing.[1] One of the reasons why the basic sanctions imposed by institutions or role-sets change slowly is that much of the 'learning' of the culture by a child is from tacit transference of traditional values and attitudes.[2]

Yet there was unquestionably a difference in the values and attitudes transmitted in child-rearing to a Henry Ford, Herbert Hoover, or Al Smith and those inculcated two generations later in Henry Ford II, John F. Kennedy, or Richard Nixon. The difference, in general, seems to be that fixed values were not as strongly implanted in the younger generations, who grew up more ready to play roles as defined by role-sets rather than by internal sanctions, that is, to try to act to please others, or to be good organization men. Much, however, has yet to be learned about the relations of child-rearing to adult character.

The leaders of the early years of the century who were welcoming release from the unscientific beliefs of the past, with confidence that new scientific truths would soon take their place, needed a general philosophy that justified experiment and change.

---

[1] F. J. Berghorn and G. H. Steere, 'Are American Values Changing?', *American Quarterly*, XVIII (Spring 1966).

[2] These attitudes or values absorbed in youth become internalized sanctions. A role-player has to reconcile his internalized sanctions with those imposed by his role-set if he is to perform satisfactorily. A product of internalized sanctions is the concept of a 'reference group', a real or imaginary authority that the actor seeks to please. In Freudian terms a reference group would be a projection from the actor's 'super-ego', or conscience, as distinct from his rational 'ego', and his subconscious source of libidinous motivation in the 'id'.

In this also William James took the lead. Borrowing from the earlier unpublished and unappreciated ideas of his colleague, Charles Pierce, James used his imposing academic influence to bring pragnatism forward in 1898, because, as he said, 'the times seemed right for its reception'.[1]

As interpreted by James and his fellow educational theorist and philosopher, John Dewey, pragmatism was not so much a new philosophy as a denial of the value of the older philosophies. It made no ultimate or metaphysical assumptions about truth, subscribed to no master metaphor symbolizing God and the universe, but rather held that truth was simply what operated predictably in a given context. In 1907, James said: 'The True is the name of whatever proves itself to be good in the way of belief, and good, too, for definite assignable reasons.'[2]

Dewey, nineteen years younger than James, applied pragmatic concepts to education, with striking effects that we shall see presently. His book, *Reconstruction in Philosophy*, published by Holt in 1920, held that philosophies were simply the ideologies found useful to the ruling élites of each period. For the enlightened age of the early tweneieth century the 'instrumentalist' or experimental approach of seeing what worked gave promise of a scientifically guided society.

Pragmatism was probably an academic statement of what men of action in the United States had always believed in an unformulated way, although they had concealed the belief, often from themselves, by asserting the values of duty and religion. Here again tensions in the role were diminished. Role-playing that was openly oriented toward maximizing utility and material satisfaction became acceptable to more and more role-sets, as editors and educators spread the pragmatic approach. It justified the almost terrifying strides the new sciences, including the social ones, were making toward discarding the values of the past millennium.

[1] See Murray G. Murphey, *The Development of Pierce's Philosophy*, Cambridge: Harvard University Press, 1961.

[2] William James, *Pragmatism, A New Name for Old Ways of Thinking*, New York: Longmans, Green, 1916, p. 76.

But disquieting ideas were about to invade this highly satisfactory world. Whereas the early pragmatism of James and Dewey tacitly assumed that social and logical tests for the operational truth of ideas could readily be performed, physicists were pursuing theories that would cast grave doubt on man's ability to perceive or understand external reality.

Although the origins of the defeat of human perception go back to the work of brilliant physicists at the University of Cambridge in the 1860s and 1870s, the men who forced the new findings on the scientific world of the twentieth century were an international group of scholars such as Albert Einstein, Max Planck, and Lord Rutherford. While all of their basic hypotheses go back to the first decade of the century, the social impact of their ideas came after World War I. Each set of findings undermined man's comprehension of a different aspect of reality. Einstein maintained that time, space, energy, and mass were not separate entities, but were relative to each other. For earthly matters the relational effects were too slight to measure, but since man thinks visually in only three dimensions, the mere four-fold character of 'relativity' meant that cosmic matters were only explicable in the symbolic language of mathematics. As Sir James Jeans, an Episcopalian physicist, put it: God was presumably a master mathematician.

Max Planck's theories of a basic minimal unit of energy interchange between electrons were the most upsetting to professionals because the hypotheses required significant revisions in mathematical logic, a shift from differential calculus to a new calculus of finite differences. But to the intellectual layman the message was again that reality was approachable only by applying exotic mathematics to meter readings and other kinds of indirect and perhaps not very reliable evidence.

Lord Rutherford's study of the structure of the atom demonstrated that human perception of solidity was a delusion. Atoms were almost entirely open space in which nuclei, electrons, and a growing family of other particles were associated with each other, with perhaps the same relative spatial relations as the sun and the planets. If in fact solid matter, rather than electrical charges, existed at all, the solids in a human body would not fill a teaspoon. What appeared to man as solid bodies with fixed forms and colours were really systems of electrical relationships.

Philosophers beat various retreats in the face of this destruction of the verbal logic on which man's systems of thought had been constructed. Dewey emphasized the social engineering aspects of his instrumental approach, or, in other words, became a social scientist rather than a philosopher, which perhaps, in truth, he had always been. Others, such as Irvin Babbit at Princeton, took the attitude that the scientific findings were extraneous to an understanding of the unchanging nature and necessities of man on earth, and promulgated a new 'humanism'. Somewhat similarly, Maurice Merleau-Ponty and Jean Paul Sartre in France restricted philosophy to the study of man's concrete perception of things in this world—a doctrine which would have influence in the United States in later decades. But the majority, following Bertrand Russell and Ludwig Wittgenstein in England, turned from cosmic or metaphysical systems of thought to the intensive study of the meaning for truth of mathematical, verbal, and other symbolic forms of logic, thus removing philosophy from the fields of knowledge interesting, or even available, to the élites which wielded social power.

The destruction of the 'reality' of the everyday world could in theory have ushered in a new age of faith. If all reality was symbolic, the symbols of religion might reclaim their superiority over those of science. But such an assumption, seriously made by a number of intellectual leaders, neglected the trend of social thought and institutions. If child-rearing and schooling had not achieved the aims of scientific or 'progressive' doctrine, they had, at least, strengthened a sceptical uncommitted attitude that could not suddenly be converted into new spiritual belief.

CHAPTER III

THE SEARCH FOR JUSTIFICATION

For a society to hold together and function, people must find some satisfactory justification for playing their role. The stronger, more all-embracing and abstract the justification, such as a belief in God's will as manifest in natural laws, the more comprehensively it will serve society. A major social problem of the western world in the middle and later twentieth century was the failure to find other comprehensive justifications to replace the earlier communal and kinship, or traditional, sanctions, or the moral belief in the duty to work. Herbert Marcuse, a German émigré to the United States and a philosopher of the deductive type, offered some penetrating critical observations on the plight of the western world in finding justifications and goals for its affluent society. He saw the élite of these nations as seeking to supplement the diminishing will to do work which technology appeared to make less necessary, by 'organizing the desire for beauty and hunger for community, the renewal of the "contact with nature", the enrichment of the mind and honours for "creation for its own sake" . . .'[1]

While losing its dogmatic authority that made work a Christian duty, and failing to institute a 'new age of faith', the church was instrumental in advancing some of the new justifications noted by Marcuse, as well as putting forward the idea of a morality based on a combination of spiritual belief and work for the welfare of society.[2] Starting early in the century, Protestant churches, which continued to enroll about two-thirds of the total

[1] Herbert Marcuse, *Eros and Civilization* (London: Sphere Books, 1969), 'Political Preface, 1966', p. 19.

[2] As will be noted shortly, Marcuse's philosophy was far from Christianity.

parishioners, began to assume social or community functions. They sought to reach the great hordes of immigrants who arrived at industrial centres each year until World War I checked the flow; to compensate through new functions for the decline in moral and doctrinal authority; to emphasize Christian duties for promoting social welfare; and to make the church a community centre for the migrants who were enlarging the cities and their suburbs.

In some of the Protestant churches the optimistic, scientific *zeitgeist* of the early century was reflected in a 'social gospel' movement that stressed work for social betterment, and hope for the increasing perfection of man. This aspect of socialized religion suffered irretrievably from the disillusioning effects of the great depression, and the succeeding decades in which war rather than peace, and mistrust rather than faith in man, became the norms. By the 1960s religious 'reform' movements were on a deeper or existential level that brought into question not only the nature of belief and of crucial aspects of the dogma and symbolism of Christianity, but also the value of authoritarian clerical hierarchies.

On the other hand, new elements had been added to the social appeal of the church in the twentieth century: the great suburban explosion enhanced the church's utility as a device for creating 'instant community'; the family church served as a means for preserving ethnic affiliations in a society in which they were disintegrating; and well-paid labour with growing middle-class attitudes began to see church membership as a social asset.[1] Polls indicated that in a vague way 95 per cent of United States citizens believed in God, but to the unprecedented two-thirds of the population who professed denominational affiliations their church probably had more social than religious significance.

Writers on theology have seen this type of religious affiliation

[1] By the twentieth century the United States had a range of occupations and income levels that could not easily be fitted into the old three-class system. Such a society of minute and uncertain gradations came to be referred to as a mass rather than class society. Yet, since it would be intolerably awkward to use precise income and occupational definitions whenever social status is referred to, for general purposes the old class language will be used.

as a belief in the 'American way of life'—a type of belonging to the community. Its effects on change could vary from a dedication to new causes, as in the earlier social gospel movement, to that of adverse sanctioning of any departure from complete conformity. The conservative-liberal polarity involved both regions and denominations, the predominantly rural areas tending to be fundamentalist in doctrine and conservative, as typified by Southern Baptists, while in the metropolitan centres the Protestant and Jewish churches were generally weak in fixed doctrinal beliefs and willing to advocate social change.

Any departure from belief in God in the direction of ultimate justification by social morality was a change from hierarchical toward equalitarian belief, but in addition, by the 1960s the clerical and lay hierarchy in the churches, as elsewhere, was under attack. This was not a serious problem for some Protestant denominations which had no official positions higher than the deacons and the parish minister, but, together with a demand for female equality, the pressure for local democratic sovereignty threatened such authoritarian structures as the Catholic church. Essentially the church as an institution was surviving by changing its social functions, and was unquestionably losing sanctioning or justifying force in the process.

Another loss of justification had arisen from a different quarter. Up to World War I economic success had been regarded, by those who shared in it, as a proof of virtue, or as its own justification. Managers exercised authority by right of the virtue of competitive energy, and workers had to accept their lot because they were morally lacking in the proper qualities. Then the new profession of industrial psychology, needed by growing bureaucracies, began to question the supremacy of economic incentives among workers. The learned specialists asserted that the desire to work was equally important, and that this depended on the atmosphere and incentives provided by management.[1]

[1] See Reinhard Bendix, *Work and Authority in Industry: Ideologies of Management in the Course of Industrialization,* New York: Wiley, 1956 (pp. 297 ff), London: Harper & Row.

It was scarcely realized at the time that this shift in the burden of responsibility for good work inevitably undermined competitive success as an ultimate moral justification. In making management responsible for the productivity of labour it created a shared social relationship not governed by any inexorable laws of God and nature. Logically management had to justify itself by the mundane and uncertain measure of ability to manage, one that any worker or government official could readily question. The development of 'cooperative unionism' in the 1920s, in which workers in the garment trade, for example, suggested to their employers how to improve managerial efficiency, was an example of the weakening of the old hierarchical authority justified by natural law.

This loss of justification by success alone had profound implications, particularly for America where material success had been most highly regarded. It brought into question the virtue of wealth and the assumed superiority of the leading citizen, whose civic activities depended on a high income. In the long run, accentuated by the experience of the Great Depression, it would shift the moral stigma of poverty from the indigent to the society that tolerated it.

As the search continued for new ultimate values to fill the void created by the weakening of divine and natural law, the economic base of western society was moving toward an unprecedented affluence. In the 1950s the economic base for the age of plenty, which Simon Patten had optimistically hailed in 1905, had finally arrived, but without the beneficent characteristics he had prophesied. The ease with which members of the upper-middle class earned large incomes and the ways in which they spent them made their children less excited by the traditional pursuit of wealth. As other careers seemed more psychologically satisfying, business appealed less to the ablest graduates and drew fewer of them into its ranks.[1]

[1] In all, the values determining the actor's choice of occupational roles and the expectations of reward had both altered sufficiently to unbalance the traditional system of institutional relations. Men played new roles, such as that of research scientist, with new motivations, and their role-sets, equally uncertain as to hierarchy of values, were hesitant in imposing positive or negative sanctions.

The young felt frustrated and angered by the failure of the ruling élites to put abundance to better use. For the first time in history the power inherent in modern technology gave man a wide range of choice that should permit the alleviation of most of the age-old material problems. They might well ask: 'With such power over, and understanding of, society why should so many roles be played in less than the best way?' But, unfortunately, 'best' might be differently interpreted by students and faculty, or presidential administrations and critical senators.

One could blame the timing of the revolt that started on the campus at Berkeley, California, in 1964 on current matters that upset American youth, such as their legally forced participation in an apparently futile and inhumane foreign policy, or the deterioration of race relations at home; but since the revolt was present in most industrial nations it obviously had deeper roots. The declarations of freedom in the slogans and placards were more than sexual emancipation proclamations; they were part of a moral rebellion against the traditional sanctions of most of the major social institutions.

The rebellion had diverse sources and was composed of highly different social groups. At one extreme were young blacks who rebelled against unemployment, poverty, and discrimination. At the other end of the social spectrum were young whites who rebelled against a materialistic heritage that made financial success rather than the good life the apparent aim of the society, and against the attitudes of parents and educators who, while lacking firm values themselves, still held that college-age youth were incapable of democratically controlling their own affairs. All the dissident groups joined in attacking the Vietnam war, which often seemed most immediately important, not only as a threat to male youth, but also as a symbol of much of what was wrong with society.

Unquestionably the number of active black or white militants within or outside the educational system were a small percentage of the total, as were those on the extreme right who stood for perpetuations of the old order by force if necessary. But polls of many types on campuses across the nation indicated a large amount of sympathy for the democratic and pacifistic aims of the left or liberal militants.

Quite aside from demands for student power and political action by universities, the situation from 1950 on was one bound to cause difficulties in adjustment to life, or, as some psychologists say, the search for identity. While in all societies parents and schools teach how to play the social roles belonging to their generation, and in fast-changing industrial societies this training has always been more or less inadequate, from 1950 on change affecting roles and institutions was unusually rapid. Yet all existing educational systems were based on the assumption that knowledge acquired in a limited period of years had high value thirty or forty years later. In the resulting confusion many students and faculty members questioned the relevance of much of the conventional learning and the structural organization of education. Whether gifted students solved such problems or not, they were nevertheless the ones who would have to 'run the society in the coming Age of Knowledge. The rebellion of youth in the colleges, therefore, had more significance for the future of society than the immediate questions of law, order, or authority or the percentage of students involved.

There was a psychological basis to the rebellion that came from giving relative leisure, either through education or unemployment, to adolescents lacking in satisfactory moral justifications for conduct. The psychoanalyst Erick Erickson contends that the hippies or flower people were those failing to progress beyond the adolescent re-enactment of the first stages of childhood.[1] Furthermore, a small group at the adolescent age-level could achieve a large response 'because it draws out and influences the latent aggravations of a majority of young people who otherwise choose only banal and transient ways of voicing dissent or displaying conflict.'[2] Yet even the normally adjusted

[1] 'Reflections on the Discontent of Contemporary Youth', *Daedalus* (Winter 1970), p. 167.
[2] *Ibid.*, pp. 156–7.

serious students found it difficult to reach a stable 'stage of identity on the terms offered by the adult world', because of the adult 'deficiencies in ethical and religious orientation', of a type which had been present in the past.[1] In other words, the failure to find satisfactory new justifications to replace the old religiously derived morality had reached a critical point. 'Many people who have no religious faith are doubly deprived today', writes the pediatrician Benjamin Spock, 'because they don't have much belief in man either.'[2]

The new philosophical ideas, concerned with assumptions about the relations of psychology and society, probably reached most of the rebellious young in verbal aphorisms rather than by study of the original authors, but the ideas provided a revolutionary philosophy which is a powerful weapon for any movement.

Ironically, the men who were basic sources of the ideas adopted by resistant youth contradicted each other in important respects. The French philosopher Jean-Paul Sartre developed appealing existential doctrines in *Being and Nothingness*, published in France in 1943, but not translated into English until 1957. Denying the force of culture or inheritance, he held that 'beings for themselves' had to make choices based upon perception of the concrete external situation.[3] Without studying the details of this conception of the need for fresh or artistic approaches to the environment, which ended in a rather pessimistic impasse between being and reality, youth could get the message that they should not be bound by the past and must decide things for themselves. At this stage Sartre was a-political and non-Marxist.

In contrast, Herbert Marcuse, in *Eros and Civilization* (1955) and subsequent writing, took off from Freud's *Civilization and its Discontents* (1949), but gave Freudian ideas more social and

---

[1] 'Reflections on the Discontent of Contemporary Youth', *Daedalus* (Winter 1970), p. 172.
[2] 'Baby and Child Care', in Michael McGiffert, ed., *The Character of Americans*, Homewood, Ill.: Dorsey Press, 1970, p. 18.
[3] See Mary Warnock, *Existentialism*, London: Oxford University Press, 1970, pp. 131-40.

political content. Marcuse saw the United States and other 'over-developed' nations as almost hopelessly bound by the continuation of 'surplus repression', a modification of human instincts once necessary in order to create an industrial society, but no longer meaningful except as a social control.[1] The affluent society was a form of fascism dominated by the big corporations and their subservient mass media. This was a control not based on force, but on 'the "social engineering" of the soul and the "science of human relations" . . .' 'The authorities', claimed Marcuse, 'are hardly forced to justify their dominion. They deliver the goods; they satisfy the sexual and aggressive energy of their subjects . . . merchandise is made into objects of the libido.'[2]

As the disease was deep-seated and the patient was unaware of it, cure was difficult. It required a complete re-ordering of the behavioural priorities built up by the repression of instincts during centuries of struggle against scarcity and want. The libido, or sexual urge, currently sublimated into work and highly conventional leisure through 'surplus repression', should be liberated by reducing repression to the 'basic' amount needed for the adequate functioning of civilization. Under the relaxation of restraints, possible if only a moderate and more evenly distributed supply of goods was required from advanced technology, the libido would energize all men's activities. Sex would also become 'polymorphous', embracing all areas of the body and 'genital supremacy' would decline.[3] Thus sex would take the place of God or work as an ultimate justification.

How the change could be brought about when most citizens were enjoying their subjugation to affluence and programmed leisure could not be spelled out. Marcuse was pessimistic about its being initiated in the overdeveloped nations, more optimistic for the reform of the developing Third World. But the appeal of this philosophy to college youth near the peak of sexuality and resistant to affluent homes, or to underprivileged ethnic groups resistant to the social system, is obvious.

Since Marxism was the one mid-twentieth-century philosophy

[1] Marcuse, *op. cit.*, p. 11.   [2] *Ibid.*   [3] *Ibid.*, p. 163.

with world-wide recognition, both Sartre and Marcuse rather tortuously related their systems to it. Sartre, in the *Critique of Dialectical Reason*, published in 1960, was able to endorse Marx by saying that the original free choice was in the conversion to Marxian belief and that thereafter one supported the perceptions of the group.[1] Marcuse found any detailed espousal of Marx equally difficult, but agreed to the practical value of his ideas by placing the discussion on a very high level of generality. He held that Marx inaugurated a mode of thinking in which the limitations of philosophy were overcome and ideas were discovered which enabled men to transform not merely thought, but social reality.[2] Yet Marcuse continually implied the weakness of class appeal in the overdeveloped nations.

Offering a quite different type of explanation from that of the new-Freudians or Marxists, and one that involved no call to youth, the philosopher and physicist Michael Polanyi contended that 'moral scepticism and moral perfectionism combine to discredit all explicit expressions of morality' and produce an 'angry absolute individualism'.[3] That is, they stimulate a search for utopias that continually dissolve upon closer examination, they create LSD dreams that cannot be realized in the real world, and hence leave the would-be moralist defeated and frustrated. There can be no question about the rise of moral scepticism. But did the amorphous New Left of the 1960s, or for that matter the 'lost generation' of the 1920s, or the intellectual and artistic communists of the 1930s, or the 'angry young men' of the 1950s all suffer from moral perfectionism?

The rebellious members of each of these generations did espouse some 'perfectionist' ideal such as the autonomy of the artist, production for use instead of profit, or world peace. Sartre's Marxian choice and Marcuse's ideal of energizing all social action from the libido were equally moral and perfectionist. The initial force of such demands was no doubt greater in the United States

[1] *Critique de la raison dialectique précedé de question de Méthode,* Paris: Gallimand, 1960.
[2] See Alastair MacIntyre, *Marcuse,* London: Fontana/Collins, 1970.
[3] *The Tacit Dimension,* Garden City: Anchor, 1966, p. 58.

than in Europe because of the exaltation of youth in traditional American culture and the relative weakness of hierarchical orders commanding ceremonial respect. But one type of perfectionism espoused by young Americans of the 1960s had peculiarly American roots: the ideal of complete non-hierarchical democracy in the operation of all institutions.

In most of the major social institutions in the 'democratic' societies, the lines of authority still went from the top down, and those who were younger or lower in the scale were expected to obey. Only in legislative representation was democracy almost a uniform rule by 1900; in the other institutions authoritarian or hierarchical structures based on the old aristocratic agrarian traditions were transmitted almost unchanged into the mid-twentieth century. As will be seen in the next chapter, elementary education became less authoritarian in classrooms, but perhaps even more so in centralized administration. Male trustees and their chosen presidents continued to control higher education, the arts were largely dominated by middlemen serving the desires of wealthy patrons, a considerable part of American Protestant churches were controlled by oligarchies of the wealthier members of their congregations, while the Catholic Church, with an absolute authoritarian, male, clerical hierarchy, had grown to be by far the largest single denomination and the most influential in politics.[1] In business the authoritarian rule from the top had been easily translated from proprietary owners to corporate executives.

Also important in creating rebellion, the older hierarchical and moralistic beliefs were often forced on the young by authoritarian parents.

Hence the more restless and perceptive members of younger generations, better educated than ever before, saw that, while they were living in political democracies, they were surrounded by the hierarchical, authoritarian institutions of the past. The fact that among students, as a whole, the democratic aspect of the rebellion tended to supersede the sexual or political (except for

[1] Abstract expressionism eliminated hierarchy altogether in the content of painting.

the Vietnam war), did not contradict Marcuse, who had predicted appeasement by granting more participation, or Polanyi, who could surely accept the demand for fully egalitarian democracy as 'moral perfectionism'. Regardless of specific philosophical views, however, the student rebellion was explicable by the pressure of new ideas on individual roles and the resulting conflict with role-sets representing authority in hierarchical institutions.

The rebellion, inspired by exciting libidinous ideologies and intensified by role conflicts and uncertainties among the most educated, spread rapidly to diverse groups of youth. Resolution was made more difficult by the simultaneous rise of the Black Power movement and the use of strong drugs. Much of the violence of the 'rock culture' of the late 1960s and early 1970s had scarcely a discernible ideological base beyond a general protest against affluent middle-class standards. Together with other rebellious groups, youth had found the vulnerability of an urban society, dependent on fantastically expensive equipment, to sit-ins and confrontations. Large crowds could quickly gather and equally quickly melt away. Repressive power was difficult to apply against those in control of costly machines, or against unseen rebels concealed behind the blank faces of city buildings. The world-wide situation had the paradoxical effect of giving a new power to minority groups in an increasingly collectivized mass society.

Since neo-Freudian and neo-Marxian prophets had no concrete political and social programmes, and since any type of moral perfectionism was logically irreconcilable with moral scepticism, the inadequately defined hopes of the young for a satisfying democratization or 'liberation' of society could not in theory be realized, and therefore one might predict a continuance of angry frustration. But philosophers and logicians deal with words, not social adjustment, and in the real world society might be closer to a more acceptable restructuring and re-sanctioning of roles than appeared to be the case in the early 1970s.

While the new democratic and libertarian aspirations awakened by science, education, and affluent industrialism were opposed by both old sanctions and vested interests, institutions continually change from what James Willard Hurst has called 'drift and cumulation', that is, from their own internal contradictions.[1] People join together for various reasons other than merely the expressed aims of the organization involved, and hence, as new situations arise, they differ with each other as to what the group should do. Changes can come as readily from the disintegration of counter-pressures—an area rather neglected by historians—as by dynamic role-playing that wins acceptance. Furthermore, members of the forces of resistance in the real world were much less organized and alert than the abstract thinkers assumed. In institutional change confusion and chance played a large part compared to calculation and planning.

While settlement of conflicts requires mutually understood definitions, these do not need the exactness of logical perfection. The world has always had to get along with approximate understandings and only partial agreements. Since most role-playing is habitual, men with greatly different motivations and knowledge can play the same role acceptably and productively, and only at times of stress or reflection do they search for their ultimate justification. For Freud and his various types of disciples, the admonitions incorporated in the super-ego during childhood, or the bidding of 'conscience', was the normal type of justification.

Yet the increasing numbers of the highly educated require some rational philosophy of ultimate justification for life and action. Can this group find a satisfactory justification for life and work in some form of the widely accepted aim of the improvement of mankind, whether by release of the libido, achievement of more complete democracy, progress to higher awareness or merely more personal and environmental welfare? Could any such goal achieve the sanctioning force of the age-old needs for survival and belief in the supernatural, or could satisfaction come

[1] All complex, institutionalized behaviour necessarily involves contradictory elements that are potential causes of change.

only with the rise of some new, perhaps aesthetically or natural-istically oriented religion?[1]

[1] In the role paradigm these are internalized sanctions that influence the perception and decisions of the role-player. If accepted by his role-sets they enter into the prescription for the social role. The problem of the Western World is one of internalizing sanctions suitable to the new social relations produced by science, technology and large populations.

CHAPTER IV

DEMOCRACY AND EDUCATION

While pre-school age is the most critical period for passing on to a child the basic types of role behaviour expected of them in society and the sanctions they are to anticipate, schooling accounts for more general ideas and attitudes regarding the world, as well as specialized knowledge or techniques. 'Learning the culture', of course, never ends and schooling is both accompanied and succeeded by the educational impact of newspapers, magazines, cinema, radio and television, collectively referred to as mass media.

Two facts have characterized formal educational systems: what is taught is prescribed by the older generation; and what is learned applies to a society that, in the industrial world, will no longer exist when the erstwhile pupil reaches his peak of social influence. In a society such as the United States, which was rapidly moving from social sanctions arising from religion and the market to those apparently based on science and institutional planning, the twenty to thirty years that generally elapsed between the end of formal education and a person's maximum social influence could be a very wide gap indeed. Herbert Hoover, for example, educated in a small-town Iowa and Oregon schools, and in the market-oriented economics of the early days of Standard University, was emotionally and intellectually ill-equipped, forty years later, to play the role of leader in the creation of a modern welfare state.

Hoover's dilemma was characteristic of a large portion of the leaders of the United States. Up to 1930, because of high rural fertility rates, most children were educated in country elementary schools, and the vast majority of such schools were single-teacher, one-room buildings. Elementary teaching, rural or urban, was poorly paid, and chiefly attracted young women during the period between the completion of their own sampling of secondary education and their marriage. In addition, it must be remembered that from the 1880s on there came to be a considerable number of influential immigrants in the society, who had received their education in Europe, usually in rural schools no better than those in the United States.

It seems remarkable that, with the levels of education generally prevailing in the late nineteenth century, and widely shared by the local and national leaders of the period from 1900 to 1940, the nation functioned as well as it did. Saving elements were the facts that continual migration was in itself an educational process, that the urban primary and secondary education received by a minority were superior to the rural varieties, and that the hereditary élite sent their children to private schools, which perhaps did no better in the way of preparation for the future, but more in the way of instilling habits of learning.

Change in the educational system started about the turn of the century from complex causes. The rise of scientific as against religious sanctions put more stress on teaching useful, factual knowledge and less on the moral training which had been the major aim of the old primary education. The idea of a scientific society, which, as we have seen, was fascinating some sectors of the élite, called for limitations on child labour in favour of considerably more schooling. The growing technology and its office controls required higher levels of clerical and supervisory training, while suburban trains and electric trolleys encouraged organization of central high schools. Thus an intellectual climate, created basically by the chicken-and-egg relationship of industrialism and science, was changing the ideas of, at least, city-dwellers who could help define educational roles.

An important early result, and perhaps in the long run one of the most important milestones in the history of education, was the passage, early in the century by all of the states, of compulsory school laws which in the large industrialized commonwealths required attendance up to the age of sixteen. For the majority this meant two or three years of secondary school, and for those with ability a strong incentive to go on and graduate.

Before the passing of compulsory school laws high school was an upper-middle-class institution regarded primarily as a preparation for college. As late as 1893, a group of ten committee chairmen of the National Education Association, all of them personally associated with institutions of higher learning, had reaffirmed the college preparatory functions of public high school curricula. But if the high school was to educate everyone and to fulfil technological needs, subjects useful to the masses must be introduced.

To meet such pressures the whole system of roles and sanctions of teachers in secondary education was bound to change drastically. As long as their students were headed for college and the learned professions, the teachers' role-set—chiefly students, parents, and school boards—shared in common a set of traditional expectations as to subjects and methods. The role was defined and, except for disciplining bored youngsters, easy to play. But the idea of teaching every youth, native or immigrant, stupid or bright, anxious to learn or held in his seat by law, soon shattered this pleasant scholastic world.

Coming at this time, compulsory education almost inevitably led to the triumph of the traditional United States value placed on utilitarianism over the equally old values ascribed to classical and religious subjects. To a degree emphasized by Richard Hofstadter, this was also a triumph of anti-intellectualism over tenuously held genteel traditions of learning.[1]

By 1911 a new study of secondary curricula, initiated by the NEA, illustrated the extent of the shift in sanctions among role-sets and in new roles expected of teachers. A committee of nine, including no college professors, reported in favour of seven main objectives for high school education: cultivation of good health; worthy home membership; training for a vocation; good

[1] See *Anti-Intellectualism in America*, New York: Alfred Knopf, 1963, Ch. XIII.

57

citizenship worthy use of leisure; proper ethical character; and 'command of fundamental processes'. Only this last awkward phrase applied to what an earlier generation had regarded as learning, and in practice the committee advised confining its content largely to knowledge of the three Rs needed by the average child. Professor Hofstadter's view that the report advocated character over mind, and conformity and manipulation over talent, made it a good example of the sanctions that had always pressed upon the playing of business roles in the United States. While in essence the report was democratic in seeking to fulfil the needs of the common man, other educational developments of the time reinforced hierarchical authoritarianism.

Beyond insistence on the need for more vocational education, there is little evidence of direct interest by businessmen in the evolving curricula, yet the dominance of the whole culture by ideas of businesslike practical efficiency impinged on the school system. Since none of the hierarchical institutions surviving from the remote past was more authoritarian in character than business organization, the boards that ran the local school systems, staffed by unpaid lawyers and businessmen, thought the road to improvement in education was through stronger and more efficient control by administrators. In the popular business language of the day, these voluntary public servants on the school boards became interested in achieving scientific management in the schools. Education was seen as a product which should be turned out with maximum efficiency, and by analogy with the factory this depended chiefly on good managers and foremen, or, applied to the school system, able supervisors and principals. Thus school administration was placed on a higher level than teaching in both prestige and salary, and remained there in 1970.

While inflation from 1900 to 1920 and the increasing spread of education tripled costs and put more pressure than ever on economically efficient administration, perfection of the school bus in the 1920s made possible a major improvement, nearly as important in the United States as compulsory secondary education: the consolidated school. Except on parts of the east coast, rural areas were not composed of clusters of small villages, but rather of farms separated by large acreages with only an occasional town. Trains and trolleys had, in part, solved the need for larger schools with more specialized faculties in the medium to large cities, but only the motor-bus could properly collect the rural children. Change, however, had to wait upon the introduction of the pneumatic tyre for trucks and buses and on joint action by associated school boards, loath to spend the necessary money. By 1930, consolidated schools were only beginning to displace small scattered elementary schools and nearly as small secondary ones. The effects on the quality of education were potentially very great, although as we shall see, diluted by adverse educational trends. The statistically measurable effect on continued secondary school attendance, between 1920 and 1940, was to raise it from three-fifths to four-fifths of the population 14 to 17 years old.

Meanwhile, the continuing trend toward utilitarian subjects, reinforced by federal aid to manual training or vocational high schools after 1917, was strengthened from a new quarter. John Dewey, the pragmatic philosopher, had always been deeply interested in child psychology and education. By 1900 he had won the leadership of an increasing group of educators who advocated studying the psychology of the young student more than the particular content of the lessons. Dewey's idea was for children to acquire knowledge by voluntarily setting up projects and then attempting to carry them out. With help from an able teacher they would thus learn the arithmetic, spelling, reading, and other skills required to solve their problems. Dewey saw this system as a substitute for learning by rote—a substitute that could be continued by more advanced projects at the secondary school level.

Obviously the system put a strain on the role of the teacher that many could not successfully bear, and it also required small classes. The result was slow progress until the end of World War I, when the Progressive Education Association was formed to spread the system, and the faculty at Teachers' College of Columbia University, then the most prestigious graduate school of education, became missionaries for the extension of Dewey's ideas considerably beyond his original aims. Influential writers on education such as Frederick Bonser and Harold Rugg combined the idea of the 'child-centred' school with advocacy of one that taught social democracy and a socially oriented morality.

While Rugg and some of his colleagues seemed too socialistic and anti-hierarchical for the conservative twenties, the emphasis on useful projects and community responsibility promulgated by the PEA had great influence. By 1938, *Time* Magazine said of the 10,000-member Progressive Education Association: 'No school in the United States has escaped its influence.'[1] In the Inglis lectures at Harvard in 1939, Charles A. Prosser, a leading school superintendent and an early advocate of vocational education which avoided controversial subjects, sounded a note that was to become dominant in the public education of the next decade. 'The important thing', he said, 'is not to teach students how to generalize, but to supply them directly with the information they need for daily living.'[2]

What Dewey had intended as a system for making difficult subjects more interesting had degenerated into a programme for eliminating them altogether. The progressives of the 1940s spoke of 'life adjustment' as the goal of education. On the basis of ranking by IQ tests, the emphasis was put on adjusting the middle 60 per cent of students: the bottom 20 per cent were regarded as unimportant academically, and the upper 20 per cent as bright enough to learn for themselves. But in many high schools there was a shortage of conventional learning for the bright ones to study. Between 1910 and 1950 academic subjects, as traditionaly defined, dropped from 80 per cent of catalogue listings in public high schools to 20 per cent. In their place came two hundred listings of new subjects such as family problems, automobile driving, and hairdressing, directly useful in community life. Steep declines in the classics and foreign languages were perhaps tolerable in this technologically engrossed society,

---

[1] *Time* (October 31, 1938), p. 31.
[2] Hotafsdter, *op. cit.*, p. 346.

but a loss of 40 per cent of the enrolment in mathematics courses was alarming.

Clearly, this accentuation of the traditional leanings toward consensus, community cooperation, and facile adjustment at the expense of the equally traditional values of inner moral vigour, hard work, and competitive drive had reached a point that menaced economic progress in a world demanding more and more difficult specialized training.[1] Studies by sociologists and psychologists underlined the danger. Judging by school readers, 'achievement motivation' had declined between 1900 and 1950.[2] Samples of third grade readers indicated that the emphasis on winning friends had increased from one-twentieth of the content to one-third.[3] John G. Cawezti finds stories for children of the 1960s largely devoted to play and creativity and lacking in regard for the old business virtues of duty, hard work, and success.[4]

The same trends had affected higher education, but to a lesser degree. Americans had almost unwittingly extended the authoritarian business structure to the spreading colleges and universities of the late nineteenth century by adopting German rather than English practices. While in the state universities businessmen had nearly always controlled the boards of trustees, in private institutions a shift on boards from ministers and other denominational leaders to lawyers and businessmen had largely taken place by 1900. Reflecting hierarchical business views of management, the new group saw their organizations through the eyes of the academic administrations. The trend toward utilitarian curricula was welcomed by the trustees, although more conservatively than in the case of the public secondary schools. The colleges still received classically trained scholars

---

[1] This process represented a shift from stronger internal role directives toward more efforts to adjust to the attitudes of major role-sets.

[2] Robin M. Williams, Jr., 'Individual and Group Values', *Annals of the American Academy of Political and Social Science* (May 1967), p. 35.

[3] Clyde Kluckholm, 'Have there been discernible shifts in American values during the last generation?', in Etting E. Morison, ed., *The American Style*, New York, Harper, 1958, pp. 171–2.

[4] *Apostles of the Self-Made Man*, Chicago: University of Chicago Press, 1965 (p. 208), London: University of Chicago Press, 1966.

from private secondary schools, had upper-middle-class traditions of learning, and were responsible for educating the professional as well as the business élite. Inspired by the early twentieth-century recognition of a 'science' of management, however, schools of business spread rapidly, until by 1930 practically every university had such a school or curriculum.

During the same period home economics, physical education, social work, and other subjects with small factual or theoretical content were added to the college curricula. But perhaps the most striking change of all, directly connected with the burgeoning of public secondary education, was the enormous spread of teachers' colleges. They had first appeared in the nineteenth century as 'normal' or teachers' training schools on the secondary level, but, in the 1920s particularly, the growing teachers' lobbies in the state legislatures achieved elevation of these schools to the college level, and also gained laws for teaching certificates requiring certain courses offered only in schools of education. Such laws, in turn, led universities to establish departments or schools of education. Thus by 1940 a very large part, if not most, of the college and university system was given over to training teachers or others in what might be regarded as techniques rather than higher learning.

In analysing how these utilitarian, anti-intellectual trends reached such extremes, it is logical to start with a consideration of the traditional norms of the culture. Anthropologists are inclined to define culture as organized diversity, or a mutual understanding that confines roles and institutions to those that appear to be in the interest of the major élite groups. Groups of influential people guide and police the sanctions that maintain these social limits. What had happened in the United States by the late 1940s can be seen as a minority, second-level élite, the professional educators, probably with the support of the mass of the population, gradually redefining educational roles and sanctions in ways that, when fully understood, were not acceptable to more powerful élite groups.

As one would expect, from the almost absurd lengths to which the trend to educate for lower levels of utility had gone, the conflict was a confusing one. Business, whose leaders, in spite of the New Deal, were still the most prestigious élite, had always favoured utilitarian education. But the world of technology in which they operated had changed to a degree that was making old practical roles disfunctional and forcing recognition of the value of abstract theoretical knowledge, particularly in the biological, physical, and some of the social sciences.

A rebellion in the late 1940s by the academic apostles of higher learning, such as Presidents James B. Conant of Harvard and James R. Killian of MIT, was supported at first by only a few business leaders, chiefly in large corporations needing scientists, some well-educated national politicians, and advanced military theorists. But as books and reports on the weaknesses of secondary education spread, and as the educational needs of the United States as a world military leader became more obvious, the middle class began to be converted. A straw in the wind was the demise of the Progressive Education Association in 1955.

How long the process of introducing, by force of argument alone, a new value on the higher learning into the historically hostile complex of American culture might have taken is hard to say, but in 1957, Russia aided the movement with the first Sputnik. Within a year influential magazines like *Time, Life,* and *Fortune,* were proclaiming the 'crisis in education'. 'The geniuses of the next generation', warned *Life,* 'are even now being allowed to slip back into mediocrity'. Soon chambers of commerce and business clubs joined the campaign for educational rigour. A nation committed to guiding the world must educate its ablest citizens to the fullest degree rather than indulge the middle masses in pleasanter adjustments to life.

Because the traditional values of a culture change only slowly, intellectual élitism, trading on fear of the Soviet Union, did not win a lasting victory. In the beginning the Pentagon and other governmental agencies were enthusiastic about grants to universities for buildings and research. But as students rebelled against scientific advances that would be used in Vietnam, and the war strained the federal budget, the alliance between higher education and the military cooled. By 1970 the leading universities were suffering financially from plants expanded by government grants of types that were no longer acceptable to many faculty members and students, while the Pentagon and conservative legislators favoured allocating scarce funds elsewhere.

The need for specialized learning, however, had, in general, been translated by the professional educators into needs for more, not necessarily better, college and university education. Increasing state appropriations went chiefly for expansion rather than improvement in quality. Because of this increase in college students the secondary schools returned part way to their old aims of college preparation, often by dividing students into two or more divisions, with parental pressures and pride counted on to make students try to keep in the upper group. Only the leading universities, aided by a great surplus of applications for admission, were able sharply to advance standards for student admission and acceptable faculty achievement.

Higher education in 1970 represented as strongly as ever the conflict in roles and sanctions between those generated by three centuries of practicality and anti-intellectualism and those required for most effective role-playing in society on a new technological level. There were some 2,500 institutions of higher learning in the United States in 1965, including 1,500 four-year colleges and 600 junior colleges, and a remainder of specialized schools of various types that issued certificates rather than professionally accredited degrees. Judged by numbers, if not academic excellence, it was preponderantly a government-controlled system, with two-thirds of the students in state, county, or municipal colleges and universities, and this public sector was growing much faster than the private.

With nearly half the 18 to 21 year-old age group in one or another of these places of higher learning, one might say that the 'life adjustment' or progressive educators had won. Education for the average student had now been extended from high school to college. With the mutual threats between the United States and the Soviet Union moving toward a stalemate of terror, and a younger generation partly opposed to military research, the support of new and higher learning appeared likely to give way again to the traditional demand to provide a practical education leading to a college degree for the average middle-class youth.

By 1960 the 'democratizing' of higher education in the direction of educating most citizens contrasted sharply with the nearly unchanged structure of hierarchical authority. As a rule, the lower the educational level of a college the more likely it was to be arbitrarily run by its administrators. Only in the more prestigious colleges and universities, whose teachers had the independence that came from recognized scholarship, had faculties been able to assert some control over general policies, but the students, who were the constituents of the system, were still not treated as competent to have power or express opinions. As noted in the previous chapter, students of the sixties often effectively protested their lack of influence by demonstrations and sit-ins. Both blacks and the 'new left' took an active part in instigating the movement, giving it an unnecessarily violent character, and making demands for preservation of neighbouring slum areas and commitment of the universities on political issues, particularly against the Vietnam War, that were more difficult to meet than those concerning internal, participative student democracy.[1] During the decade, however, the student's movement in many places brought them representation on departmental, faculty, and university committees, and in a few instances on boards of trustees. As might have been expected, the major universities, in general, granted these demands more readily than those where administrators had always ruled supreme. By 1970 universities had become much more alert to their relations with their urban environments, and had taken the first steps toward democracy by consultation and consensus. American students seemed also to have assumed a greater political and social responsibility, but whether these attitudes would survive the disappearance of the

[1] Yet, since the attack was on old and deeply entrenched institutions of control, the new student roles might not have been accepted without a certain amount of forceful action.

65

immediate issues that had helped to give them birth, such as the Vietnam War, remained to be seen.

Regardless of the democratic quality of its educational system, the United States of 1970 represented, for the first time in history, a nation in which a majority of its younger citizens, and nearly all of the most influential ones, had from 14 to 19 years of formal education. If democracy depended on an educated electorate, it had a better chance for survival and improvement than ever before.

CHAPTER V

COMMUNICATION AND COMMUNITY

The discussion of the rise of new knowledge and its effect on the attitudes or values expressed in roles has largely been concerned with basic forces making for change in institutions. The search for justification beyond the evasive 'this is the way we do things' was essentially a quest for new directives or prescriptions to control role-playing. In the present chapter, dealing with mass media for disseminating information and amusement, the emphasis is more on the forces operating for conformity than on those making for change. Like the tacit parental attitudes transmitted in child-rearing, mass media, necessarily controlled in the United States by the business élite, were forces for perpetuation of a satisfactory politico-social *status quo*, as well as for the enchancement of material wants.

Yet any type of information or entertainment carries messages not planned by its sponsors and serves to reshape institutions in unanticipated ways. Furthermore, the impact depends on the stability of the culture at any given time, or how widely the existing institutions are accepted as justifiable. A criticism of presidential policy, for example, could have a considerably stronger force for institutional change in the 1960s than in the 1920s.

That the messages of mass media had become an inextricable part of the consciousness of the average American was illustrated by the reputed spending of two hundred million dollars, with television as the largest cost, on the 'off-year' election campaigns of 1970.[1]

[1] *Time* (November 23, 1970), p. 13.

This was not only an arresting example of the importance which these experts in political opinion attached to the influence of electronic media, but also suggested a menace to one aspect of democracy in politics. The oligarchical principle of government by men who could command wealth seemed to be returning from its reported exile in the days of Andrew Jackson. This threat to the general rise of the principles of participative democracy forced new consideration of the importance and control of mass media, generally defined as newspapers, magazines, cinema, television and radio.[1]

At the beginning of the century daily or weekly newspapers were the chief, and among the lower class the only, medium read by adults. Children and adolescents read schoolbooks and juvenile fiction, although comic strips were leading them to open that section of the papers. The dailies were chiefly supported by advertising, and had always to be careful that their handling of the news did not offend local business. In addition, every big city daily was itself a large business run for the benefit of a proprietor or stockholders. By 1915, except for a few metropolitan dailies which had their own corps of correspondents, national and foreign news was supplied by three press associations.

The number of daily newspapers reached a peak of 2,500 in 1915, and then gradually declined to about 1,700 in 1970. The drop in numbers was not caused so much by the competition of the new media for disseminating news, such as the radio after 1920, as it was by the spread of chains and mergers. By 1930, led by Scripps-Howard and Hearst with some 25 papers each, some fifty chains owned nearly 300 dailies. The tendency of successful papers, whether owned by chains or individuals, was to buy their local competitors and thus secure a monopoly position with advertisers. The old ideal of politically partisan competing papers was superseded by that of one journal which was in tune with the attitudes of local business. By 1950 very few small cities had

[1] For the thesis that control of communication is control of society see Harold A. Innes *The Bias of Communication*, Toronto: University of Toronto Press, 1951.

competing dailies, and only about half of the cities with over 100,000 population had such competition.

As would any system of ownership, this business pattern of control introduced its biases into the news. Up to 1930, at least, public relations items from advertising agencies showing their clients or their industries in a favourable light were regularly printed in the news columns of even the leading papers. Since only a quarter of the advertising revenue was national, local news had a chamber of commerce or booster character; what was good for the city was played up; what was likely to hurt local business was carried on back pages or not at all. As the newspaper-owner Roy Howard sagely remarked: 'I do not subscribe to the general idea that news and opinion are two separable elements.'[1] Before World War II lower-class ethnic groups, for example, were not considered newsworthy save to provide warnings against crime. Yet, within the pro-business, nativist biases of the culture many reporters thought they wrote objectively. Their language could be colourful, they could take sides on issues regarded according to business and religious norms as debatable, but they must stay within the rules of the game and not offend advertisers.

As time went on and newspapers suffered from the competition of other media, it was found helpful to circulation to give readers of monopolized news a variety of conflicting views by syndicated columnists whose opinions could always be disavowed by the individual paper.

Magazines, like newspapers, were businesses dependent on advertising revenue, but there were some differences. The appeal both to the public and to advertisers was generally on a national basis, and the lower cost of staffing and printing a weekly or monthly journal permitted both small magazines aimed at special audiences and those supported by private subsidy in place of advertising. Therefore, news and comment that went beyond the norms of the culture was far more likely to be found in a magazine than in a daily newspaper. From the standpoint of the

[1] Alfred M. Lee, *The Daily Newspaper in America*, New York: Macmillan, 1937, p. 537.

population as a whole, magazines of opinion had a small audience before World War II, and although with affluence and more education in the 1960s the circulation of magazines such as *Time* rose into the millions, the readers were chiefly middle or upper class. The news weeklies, both generalized and specialized, tended, therefore, to give uniform businesslike opinions the added strength that an internal sanction gains from continual reinforcement.

But the relating of news and opinion in papers and magazines to the operation of the role system and social change is best postponed until the somewhat different character of cinema, radio, and television has been historically surveyed. The coming of such electrically operated media marked a radical change from print and an equally radical advance in the influence of business.

Perhaps the United States was particularly vulnerable to the types of influence exerted by the new media. The feeling of community was relatively weak in the United States because of continual migration, and, as much of the population came to live in large, impersonal cities, had been partly satisfied in the nineteenth century by the creation of neighbourhood groups, ethnic and fraternal associations, and other bonds of friendship or face-to-face recognition. As was seen in Chapter III, among neighbourhood organizations there was an increasing reliance on the church as an agency for absorbing newcomers into a meaningful whole.

Alongside these older efforts at community through physical proximity, the electrical media sought, for business reasons, to build a national community in which all might share in the lives and actions of real or fictional characters. One need not agree with extreme views on the effects of the cinema in order to affirm that Mary Pickford became 'America's Sweetheart' through many appearances in the movies, or that Franklin D. Roosevelt became a friend to millions of Americans by radio, as no president could have done earlier, or that the cast of a television show could become intimates who entered the home one or more times a week, and whose activities were discussed with friends and neighbours.

In addition to their function of creating a new type of community built around the activities of characters approved by business interests, the electrical mass media of the twentieth century came to be powerful influences for a uniform national culture, a culture not specifically planned to satisfy business needs, but one subject to subtle business influences and censorship, since these media reached children as much as, if not more, than adults, they gained enormously as social conditioning forces. In 1953 only two-fifths of American homes had television; by 1970 nearly all had sets. As cinema, radio, and television came to have a life-long psychological influence, contributions of the older media, such as newspapers, magazines, and books, probably tended to decline. Undoubtedly, all people caught up, willy-nilly, in the national community of advertising and entertainment became more conditioned by all types of mass media in comparison to personal contacts and direct experience (even the consumption of paper for newsprint grew 150 per cent from 1945 to 1970). They came to live, that is, more vicariously.[1]

The conditions of production for the electrical media inevitably gave those who supplied the money greater control. Newspapers and magazines were published to make revenue from advertising supplying 'objective' information or other material contributed by only partially controlled authors. Cinema shows, in contrast, could be deliberately fabricated by the studios to fit the market. In the first case there was a certain inevitability in the material that had to be carried: major events, though unfavourable to the publishers, that would not be suppressed by all journals, had to be noted by all, and popular authors were published without much fear of the effects on advertisers, while in the case of the cinema there were no demands on content other than legality and the effect on profits. Hence as soon as cinema came to be produced by a few large, theatre-going corporations, the product became standardized around certain recognized and economically desirable

---

[1] This meant with less of the reinforcement in role-playing that comes from positive, face-to-face sanctions. Impersonally or remotely sanctioned ways of behaving could be more readily altered, or manipulated by a new external force.

trends in public taste. The process, while it involved the arts as an essential ingredient, was, from the business standpoint, much like automobile design, or other industrial art forms, created primarily to sell goods.

As in automobile production, the industry began around 1900 with a number of competing small enterprises, among which consolidations began in 1908. By 1930, except for a few large cities, the cinema had nearly eliminated other forms of professional theatrical entertainment, and for the next twenty years the industry was dominated by a few combinations which both produced films and owned first-run theatres where the pictures were shown. In 1948 federal anti-trust action led to a United States Supreme Court decision which divorced theatre-owning from production, forbade block booking (compulsory taking of all of a line of pictures from a given producer), and left it to the lower courts to work out details. As a result of ensuing court decisions the industry came to have a rather complicated business set-up, in which each of the major producers often established a special subsidiary corporation for an important picture. In this way stars could be paid partly in stock that would give both them and the other shareholders a return subject to capital gains rather than income taxes.

But no matter how the business end of production was organized it still controlled what was to be produced. The relation of the management of the production studio to writers, directors, and actors was much the same as that of the sponsors of radio or television programmes. With the cost of full-length features running from hundreds of thousands of dollars to many millions, the production manager could not afford to indulge any idle interest in art or education at the possible expense of revenue from sales. He was accountable to a board of directors, which often included bankers who felt responsible for the financial welfare of the film. Only by chance would important members of the board of directors or stockholders have an interest in the cinema as a form of art. As the famous director Rouben Mamoulian remarked in the 1930s: 'The picture industry is no different from the underwear business, for example, it is completely governed by the law of supply and demand.'[1]

As registered by box-office returns, demand appeared to be for romantic plots representing over-simplified solutions to human problems, usually worked out by people with a very high standard of living. The support of materialistic or businesslike values was a circular process. The audience of a culture that esteemed material success created a demand for pictures that showed the life of the rich, and such pictures, in turn, reinforced the desire to achieve such a standard of living. For those who knew they no longer had a chance to acquire wealth, pictures could provide escape and enjoyment. The elements continually slighted in this fairly stable adjustment to the market were the serious exploration of human personality or complex social problems. The Hollywood slogan was: 'This is an entertainment industry, if you have a message send it by Western Union.'[2]

Although films were produced by large business firms, their content, good or bad, had to be supplied by authors, directors, and actors who might somewhat influence the picture by personal views on religion, romance, partisan politics or a number of other social interests. As long as such opinion was popular at the box office it would be tolerated by the producer. In radio and television, however, there was a much closer tie between specific content and the business reasons for production than existed between either authors and publishers, or artists and motion picture producers. Each single production using an hour of prime radio or television time cost a great deal of money, and the businessmen paying the physical costs wanted to be as sure as possible that the content would create a favourable and profitable image for their company and its products.

The electronic media also gave advertising a new effectiveness. From 1900 to 1920 all advertising had cost an average of 4 per cent of the gross national product; from 1950 to 1970, probably

[1] Charles A. and Mary Beard, *America in Mid-Passage,* New York: Macmillan, 1938, p. 594.
[2] Martin Steinman, ed., *Film and Society,* New York: Scribner, 1964, p. 51.

73

a greater influence was achieved at a cost that ran under 3 per cent. Or, seen another way, in 1965 national television advertising, for all its effectiveness, cost less than one-fifth of all advertising placed in newspapers.[1] One could read magazines or newspapers, for example, without paying attention to the surrounding advertising; but to avoid absorbing the sponsor's message on radio or television required special equipment.

Aided by the new media from 1930 on, advertising became, in the view of David Potter, the major institution produced by American 'abundance'—one ranking with education and religion as an agency for social control.[2] But this new institution differed fundamentally from those of learning or religion in that it lacked social goals other than maintenance of orderly and profitable markets. 'It is this lack of institutional responsibility,' writes Professor Potter, 'this lack of inherent social purpose to balance social power, which . . . is a basic cause for concern about the role of advertising . . . to fix the attention but not to engage the mind' is a precise statement of the advertiser's formula.[3] The sponsor wanted to attract as wide an audience as possible, which meant a programme that would play upon easily aroused emotions, but would not produce any 'controversial' or divisive ideas. On the principle that one tends to like what one knows, a net result was undoubtedly a strengthened attachment to the 'American way of life' or the 'religion' of 'Americanism'.

In addition to these rather obvious impacts the viewer or listener had a feeling of immediate physical contact with the speaker or actor. While still at home, he was nevertheless in a live show, a part of ongoing events; he could share in the excitement of unforeseen happenings and the triumphs of a successful performance. The man on the electronic waves was, after all, addressing each one of his audience personally, and they might even reply by letter or phone in such a way as to influence

[1] 'Electronic' refers to the use of vacuum tubes or transistors that can greatly magnify weak electrical impulses.

[2] David Potter, *People of Plenty: Economic Abundance and the American Character*, Chicago: University of Chicago Press, 1964, 167 ff.

[3] *Ibid.*, 177, 182.

subsequent performances. In addition, Marshall McLuhan thinks it important that sensory apparatuses different from those used in reading were called into play in receiving radio or television.[1]

The radio phase of 'the electronic revolution' occurred rapidly. Between August of 1920 when a radio station owned by the Detroit *News*, a daily paper, began broadcasting special features, and the beginning of 1923 nearly 600 transmission stations were set up. About 40 per cent were owned by radio or electrical dealers or manufacturers, over 10 per cent each by educational institutions and news publications, and about 5 per cent by department stores.[2] While in 1920 American Telephone and Telegraph, General Electric, and Westinghouse had entered into a cross-licensing agreement, A.T. & T. with its exclusive rights to wire transmission, was really in control. For a while the telephone company thought of establishing a national system of broadcasting stations, but business resistance to such a monopoly was strong and A.T. & T.'s station, WEAF, in New York was not making money. Consequently the company, in 1924, offered licences to use wires to the hundreds of local stations, already guilty of patent infringement, and two years later sold WEAF to Radio Corporation of America, a subsidiary of General Electric. RCA organized the National Broadcasting Company with 24 stations, and by 1929 the three major networks, which were to dominate broadcasting from then on, were competing for the big advertising accounts, and agencies were advising a moderate investment in radio time.[3]

Up to this point radio programmes had consisted primarily of news, sports and popular music, and many stations, maintained in order to hold a position in the broadcasting field, had been losing money. The profits had been in the sale of equipment. Now, in spite of the deepening depression, broadcasting became

[1] Marshall McLuhan, *Understanding Media*, New York: McGraw-Hill, 1964, 2nd edn, Signet Books (p. 64); London: Routledge, 1964; Sphere, 1967.
[2] William Peck Banning, *Commercial Broadcasting Pioneer*, Cambridge, Mass.: Harvard University Press, 1946, pp. 132–3.
[3] Orrin E. Dunlap, Jr., *Radio and Television Almanac*, New York: Harper, 1951, pp. 83 ff.

profitable. Advertising agencies offered sponsors programmes by the stars of the night clubs, theatres and movies, and the station rates for prime evening time shot upward. A prediction made by two writers in 1925, that 'more attention will be given to the contents of political speeches which will be heard in the calm of the fireside', was fulfilled by Franklin Roosevelt both as Governor of New York (1929-1933) and as President.[1]

The desires of the network, the agency and the sponsor both to sell a product and to hold an audience in competition with other shows had important results. It meant that, in reality, the networks such as ABC, CBS or NBC surrendered control of programming to advertising agencies and business sponsors. In the liberal climate of the 1930s, the stations merely watched to see that no offensive language or remarks were made and that opinions expressed were within the range normally expected in the society. The agency wanted the programme to be entertaining and appealing, and not weighed down by any excess baggage of serious or dull discussion. The sponsor had similar interests but, in addition, wanted nothing said that might, even indirectly, reflect adversely on his product or his industry. A cigarette company, for example, censored the use of Jerome Kern's great song hit 'Smoke Gets In Your Eyes', and a milk company found a menace to sales in the song 'The Old Oaken Bucket'.[2] Selectivity based on popularity with listeners was made more rigorous by the rise of programme rating services from 1929 on, which, first on the basis of recall by listeners and later through sampling by 'coincidental' telephone, estimated the size of the audience.[3] In 1956 such testing developed the interesting fact that both adults and teenagers on Iowa farms that had television sets spent more time watching them than city-dwellers.[4]

[1] Samuel A. Rothafel and Raymond Yates, *Broadcasting, Its New Day*, New York: Century Co., 1925, p. 88.

[2] Morris L. Ernst, *The First Freedom*, New York: Macmillan, 1946, p. 159.

[3] See Mathew N. Chappell and C. E. Hooper, *Radio Audience Measurement*, New York: Stephen Day, 1944. The effectiveness of magazine and newspaper advertising was also measured by these agencies.

[4] Leo Bogart, *The Age of Television: A Study of Viewing Habits and the Impact of Television on American Life*, New York: Frederick Unger, 1956, p. 67.

Radio, and after World War II television, grew steadily in relation to other advertising media. While total expenditures for national advertising in relation to national income was declining slowly in the 1920s and rapidly in the 1930s, to reach by 1943 the lowest point in the twentieth century, national advertising over ratio was growing in dollar expenditures, and in percentage of both national income and total advertising outlays. It reached its peak in the late forties. In 1965, advertising expenditures were: 6 per cent for radio; 17 per cent for television; 8 per cent for magazines; 15 per cent for direct mail; 30 per cent for newspapers and the remaining 24 per cent in miscellaneous special forms. A large part of all but magazine and television advertising was local. Only 30 per cent of television advertising was on networks, but of this about one-third came from a dozen big companies.[1] This fact led a critic to complain that network television 'is operated in the specific interest of certain patent medicine makers, soap chemists and tobacco curers.[2] Another protested the tendency to lead the viewer to a kind of village-like conformity to the social norms of urban big business.

The types of control over television content, exercised solely for advertising reasons, were superficially, at least, a-political and amoral. But the great anti-Red scare from 1947 to 1953 demonstrated that business controls could also be manipulated by organized minority groups working for personal or political ends. In these instances, as usual, the decisive influence was exercised under the rubric of 'the demands of the market', but this did not lessen the force of the decisions as an example of effective control of the programmes.

In 1947 some ex-FBI men sought to profit from the rising fear of communism by forming American Business Consultants and publishing a paper, *Counterattack*, both designed to expose subversive activities in the United States. As the Red scare waxed half a dozen major companies employed American Business

---

[1] Figures from McCann-Erickson, Inc., quoted in Bogart, *op. cit.*, pp. 178–83.
[2] Albert N. Williams, *Listening*, Denver, Colorado: University of Colorado Press, 1948, p. 75.

Consultants to ferret out communists, and in 1951 the consultants published *Red Channels*, listing 151 alleged subversives in the business of entertainment. The bases for inclusion in the list were fantastic, such as having attended a single meeting at which communists were present, and the reports were often completely erroneous.

Coupled with the fears aroused by Senator Joseph McCarthy, the effects on cinema, radio, and telvision were alarming. Agency and network executives came to the conclusion that 'controversial people are bad for business', while sponsors took the position that they must protect the interests of their stockholders.[1] Producers submitted the names of writers, directors, and actors to agencies for investigation and were subsequently informed by phone with a simple 'Yes' or 'No' for each name. A banned actor was said to be 'unavailable', and of 5,000 names submitted in one year to the security staff of a large advertising agency over 1,500 were rejected. The persecution, which was largely over by the middle fifties, drove most black-listed artists to other ways of earning a living, and a few to alcoholism, drugs, or suicide.

The whole episode presents an arresting example of the tenuous place of freedom of opinion in electronic media. A few businessmen were either conscientious fanatics or publicity-seekers, but the great majority were simply trying to adjust their policies to what seemed to be required by the market. Yet, when such a policy led to questioning appearances by Eleanor Roosevelt or Pearl Buck, or eliminating the word 'peace' because it sounded communistic, adjustment to the market seemed dangerous in an industry 'affected with a public interest'.

The social dilemma was that, because of the capital equipment involved and the cost of production, electronic media seemed bound to be controlled by financially strong agencies, and such groups inevitably would have special interests to serve. Hundreds of business firms might, in fact, exercise a safer type of control

[1] Eric Barnouw, *The Golden Web: A History of Broadcasting in the United States*, Vol. II *1933–1953*, New York: Oxford University Press, 1968, p. 264.

in some respects than government, because on many issues the business group represented differing viewpoints. Private enterprise also produced many competing channels some of which might cater to minorities. To be effective in specific cases, power has to be exercised by individuals, not by vaguely defined groups. An individual with governmental authority could wield control in his own interest, whereas conflicting business groups could not. Thus, although the degree of control in the common interest of profit and the sale of products was practically absolute, in matters of method and content there was considerable leeway.

In spite of the fact that all the companies involved in producing national television programmes were very large, they were also highly competitive for public favour. Hence, while they might be unduly sensitive to well-organized minorities, they were also responsive to broad shifts in social attitudes. Hard-headed executives might not have much emotional involvement with civil rights, for example, but they knew in the 1960s that it was good business to have some blacks on the shows they sponsored. Looked at another way, if actual events influenced the majority of people in a certain direction, sponsors were loath to offer opposition unless the movement was directly menacing to the business system.

Theoretical study of the processes involved in the formation or alteration of opinion, however, casts doubt on the direct effects of mass media in bringing about 'any sudden or radical change on subjects that matter'.[1] Mass media may inform, but in general a person will not accept the idea or change his role-playing until he has tested it by conversation with influential people in his role-set. Since such 'influentials' generally represent the existing social norms, they are likely to react favourably only to changes in the direction of existing roles and institutions.[2] This recognition of the role of intervening variables between reception of an

---

[1] Elihu Katz, *International Encyclopedia of the Social Sciences*, New York: Free Press, 1968, Vol. IV, p. 149.

[2] Role-players may react favourably to one type of authoritarian control and adversely to another. Institutions, as already noted, organize people with many conflicting purposes into common behaviour for a certain function.

idea and change in behaviour does not contradict Professor McLuhan and others on the strong potential influence of electronic or 'cool' mass media, but it makes the results, judged solely by the message, indeterminate. Will it be generally enough accepted to overcome the previous norms in personal discussion and role-playing? Will it be adversely sanctioned and soon forgotten, or will it have some effect unforeseen by the promulgator, as when Senator Joseph McCarthy lost his public influence through over-exposure of his unpleasant personality?

There is a potent continuous influence, however, on a more basic level than changes in or reinforcement of ideas based on current events and day-to-day opinion. In fact, except for news broadcasts and a very few variety shows that are particularly popular, programmes are not involved in forming controversial opinion. Their chief influence is in reinforcing the customs and habits of an acquisitive, competitive society; in reinforcing achievement motivation, desire for physical luxuries, success by forceful, or occasionally violent, behaviour, and the other traits that have traditionally made up the 'American way of life'.

Thus the electronic media joined the expanded educational network and the church in reinforcing the historic roles and institutions of the culture. But since the institutional relations they sought to reinforce, in the interests of the dominant élites, were usually those formed in an earlier period, they were bound to be dysfunctional for some people and hence liable to change.

CHAPTER VI

THE DUAL REVOLUTION

Information and tacit personal influences change the intentions of a role-player or convince his role-sets of the desirability of new ways of doing things. Technological innovations, on the other hand, while necessarily stemming from intellectual origins, ultimately change social roles by altering the physical environment in which men act. The relatively few inventions that lay at the base of automotive and electrical development evolved into myriad changes in ways of living and countless new roles and institutions. The innovations of the dual revolution constitute so much of the physical basis of modern life that even a brief summary of them becomes complex.

Their popular heroes, Thomas A. Edison in electricity and Henry Ford in motors, are in the front rank of men who are symbols of the technological precocity of the United States. They were typical of ingenious Americans of their day in contributing, in quite different ways, to technology, not science. Edison, while a reader of the work of scientists, was in practice a patient seeker for practical adaptations.[1] Ford was little interested in either reading or science as such, but obsessed as an artist with the design of machinery. 'Machines are to a mechanic', he said in his *Memoirs*, 'what books are to a writer.' On another occasion he said: 'The Ford plant offers more resources for practical education than most universities.'[2]

Edison was a generation older than Ford, and his important electrical devices, such as the incandescent lamp and its installation

[1] See Matthew Josephson, *Edison*, New York: McGraw-Hill, 1959, Maidenhead, Berks.; McGraw-Hill, 1963.
[2] Henry Ford, *My Life and Work*, Garden City: Doubleday Page, 1926, pp. 24, 212.

in large cities, had their initial effects before 1900. By that date a whole range of electrical developments by Edison and others, including large generators for regional electric power, were in operation. Therefore the electrical revolution started considerably earlier than that stemming from the internal combustion engine, but the electrical was a two-phase change, and the second and probably more important part, involving 'electronic' devices, only began when automotive transportation was relatively mature. While our interest here is in effects on social change, it is necessary for a background to sketch briefly the chronological advance of the new technology and its immediate physical consequences.

From 1900 to 1930 electrical equipment, including central power stations, urban and suburban lighting and electrical communication, absorbed more capital than any other type of industry and rivalled railroad investment of the late nineteenth century in its relative share of the gross national product. By the end of the first decade of the century some manufacturers were relying on electricity for power, practically all cities had electric light, and businesses and middle-class homes had telephones. By the end of the third decade electrical power was rapidly displacing steam, and failure to have electric light or phone in urban areas was a sign of poverty. In rural regions, however, the cost of stringing wires for miles to serve a few consumers was too high for either privately owned utilities or customers to bear. Only about ten per cent of farms had electricity, and much of this came from small private generators.

From the start the large capital needed for electrical installations, and the relative stability of the securities of such public utilities, had led the biggest investment banking houses into the field, as initial organizers and guiders of the industry. Street railway and power companies were partly brought under consolidated ownership through holding companies, General Electric and Westinghouse dominated the manufacture of equipment through pooled patents, and A.T. & T., by patents, mergers and leases, monopolized long-line telephone service.

No previous major industry had moved so quickly from pioneer beginnings to giant companies. The impact of these changes on roles and institutions may be seen more completely when combined with the nearly contemporary rise of automotive transportation.

In spite of late entry into the competition, with no motor-cars commercially produced before those of Charles Duryea in 1896, there were a number of reasons why the United States was most likely to forge ahead in the development of an inexpensive and reliable vehicle. No other industrial nation had such a scattered population and consequent need for faster transportation over distances of from ten to a hundred miles; no other nation had as large and prosperous a middle class that could afford such a luxury; the period from 1897 to 1913 was one of general prosperity which permitted, except for 1908, a rapid growth in the market; and, although not unique in this respect, the United States had unusually well-developed machine shops, bicycle and wagon works, and other 'suppliers' that made 'production' of an automobile chiefly the assembling of prefabricated parts.[1]

Since American rural roads, and even most city streets, were not suitable for automobiles the immediate need for the spread of this innovation was government investment in paved highways. As this continued to be the case, even when the industry was mature, the result was a mixture of private enterprise manufacturing goods whose use depended on government-owned facilities. In contrast to the privately owned railroads of the nineteenth century, public ownership of the equipment necessary for the use of both motor vehicles and aeroplanes was in accord with the apparently inevitable trend of advancing industrialism to make use of government. More than in most 'mixed' industries the division of functions in automobiles was sharp; there was no production of vehicles by government and no ownership of through roads by private business. Of the two sectors of the industry, roads, with an annual capital investment of over a

[1] See James J. Flink, *Reception of the Automobile, 1895–1910*, Cambridge, Mass.: The MIT Press of Cambridge, 1970.

billion dollars a year by 1920, represented much the larger capital commitment, and one for which there was a continuous unmet demand.

Henry Ford, who was to play the most important innovating role in passenger-car production, combined in his personality an obsessive emotional interest in powered transportation over roads and an early conditioning outside the culture of urban-industrialism. He remembered his excitement when, as a boy, he saw a threshing machine being slowly hauled along the road by steam power. Perhaps rebellion against his prosperous Michigan farming family also entered into his behaviour—as usual the historian knows too little about individual childhoods to pass judgment.[1] At all events, he stoutly resisted family efforts to interest him in agriculture and took jobs in Detroit for, as he recalled later, the express purpose of learning about transportation machinery. Although his formal education consisted of a one-room school-house up to the age of 17 and a brief term at a business 'college', not marks of intellectual precocity, by the 1890s he became the chief 'engineer' of the Detroit Edison Company. During this same decade he continued to experiment in a well-equipped private workshop on the perfection of a road vehicle. The quality he demonstrated in some fifteen years of experimentation was preoccupation with the problem, not ability at its solution.

His entry into the automobile business was made possible in 1903 by a chance event, his sister's marriage to James Couzens, a business-man familiar with company promotion. The total capital of what was initially a four-man partnership is said to have been less than $30,000, and for the first five years of operation the company achieved only a moderate success, a factor that aided Ford and Couzens in getting rid of the other partners.

What Ford contributed to the role of automobile manufacturer is well known. Why he, rather than someone such as David Buick or Ransom E. Olds, shaped the role in this way is impossible

[1] For a psychological approach see Anne Jardim: *The First Henry Ford: A Study in Personality and Business Leadership*, Cambridge, Mass.: MIT Press of Cambridge, 1971.

to answer. Some factors worth considering are that Ford's country background made him very much aware that fear of expensive or locally unavailable repairs was probably the major factor retarding the spread of automobiles in rural areas. He was aided by his lifelong desire to simplify things (which was to involve him later in social difficulties), and the fact that, coming into the industry late, after long and rather unsuccessful experimentation he had, perhaps, a novel view of its problems.[1]

Just how much Ford personally initiated, and how much depended on his associates, is elusive. All will agree that he made the major managerial decision to concentrate on a single model that would be adequate in speed and power, simple to repair, and as inexpensive as these qualities would permit, but, having made this decision, he left actual design to able young engineers with whom he frequently conferred. The elements that went into the Model T were adaptations of widely known devices. Perhaps there was a large element of chance in the fact that the whole exceeded the sum of its parts, and that a relatively untapped market existed which soon gave Ford an advantage in costs from his scale of operations—an advantage which he pursued vigorously through price-cutting.

His two other major innovations may well have sprung inevitably from the effects of the first. Since Ford distrusted urban financiers he would neither borrow money nor sell securities to outsiders. This meant that the company had to grow from reinvested earnings, and as demand soared this became a severe constraint. Again Ford set able engineers to studying how to get more product from the same men and equipment, and at the end of 1913 they came up with a plan to adapt the automated assembly line, widely used in bottling plants, to automobiles. Here again the results vastly exceeded expectations. The productivity of labour in the assembly operations was increased sevenfold, and the public hailed Ford as having introduced mass production.

[1] In the case of innovators in roles, such as Ford, fresh perception of the situation is of the highest importance, but this perception is still culturally as well as internally conditioned.

Certainly the two innovations—Model T and the automobile assembly line together—constituted a minor technological revolution, yet neither involved anything except prolonged, systematic thought by technicians on recognized problems.[1]

The possibilities inherent in work paced by management, through the speed of the line, may have led Couzens to suggest to Ford that they could profit from hiring and retaining only the ablest workers, and the way to procure them was by paying more than anyone else. The publicity attached to the announcement, in the depressed year of 1914, that Ford would pay a five-dollar-a-day minimum, almost double that of the rest of the industry, emphasized that a Ford employee should be able to buy a Ford car. Again the public hailed Ford for acting on the emerging principle that only high mass-consumption could support mass-production. Had Ford died at that time he would have been a great national and probably an enduring world hero. Unfortunately for his reputation he lived to a cantankerous old age, repeatedly demonstrated a failure to understand modern society, promoted anti-Semitism, and developed a rigid, dictatorial personality.

In the 1920s, with Ford no longer a leader, motor-car technology and the industry reached relative maturity. Powerful engines, enclosed bodies, soft tyres, four-wheel brakes, and even an automatic transmission, achieved everything except unified welded bodies and frames that were to place automobiles on a technically static plateau for the next forty years. The used car market, planned obsolescence of superficial design, instalment selling, strict factory supervision of dealers and monopolistic competition, led by Chrysler, Ford and General Motors, also established a lasting pattern in the industry. Not only did automobile buying greatly increase spending for consumer durables, but some of the motor companies joined the electrical group as suppliers of new electrified household equipment. From a level

[1] For social change the question whether an invention or innovation is new is, of course, unimportant. It is not the mechanism that counts, but its effects on roles, sanctions and institutions. The cheap Model T was a major force in making the automobile, from many standpoints, a central institution of American society.

of 6 per cent of national income in the first decade of the century, relative consumer spending for durables had doubled by the third decade, reaching a percentage that had not been substantially exceeded by 1970.

Trucks and buses also initiated changes in the 1920s that were greatly to alter American society. Here the critical technological element was the big, reliable pneumatic tyre that enabled these heavy vehicles to use poorly surfaced roads. By the end of the decade trucks were cutting into the local, small-lot freight business of the railroads, and buses were leading to the abandonment of trolley tracks, but these were only portents of more sweeping changes to come, as the whole society became built around automotive transportation.

The Great Depression of the 1930s and suspension of manufacture for civilian use during World War II held back the revolutionary social impact of passenger cars, trucks, and buses until the fifties and sixties, and to a lesser degree of express highways, which were not seen by either Hoover or Roosevelt as an important stimulant to private capital investment. Not until the late forties was a major effort made to provide the wider concrete roads that could add greatly to the efficiency of automotive transportation and move factories to new locations. With the development of the Eisenhower programme of free interstate highways, 90 per cent financed by Congress, from 1958 on, and the earlier growth of state toll roads, all major cities in the more populous parts of the nation became connected by one or more four-lane roads.

Meanwhile, in public transport, the bus had made the electric trolley a rarity, to be seen only in the largest cities, and short-distance train travel unprofitable for the railroads. Between 1945 and 1960 the railroads also found it impossible to protect long- or middle-distance passenger service from the aeroplane, and all types of freight, except long-haul carload lots, from the truck. Since the trains were pulled by either diesel or centrally fed electric locomotives, one could call the triumph of electricity and the internal combustion engine in the field of transportation complete.

Our concern here, however, is not with the details of the machines, but with the impact on social change. Two different types of effect were present: that arising from gradual changes in the physical environment which involve new attitudes and means of living; and that of changing occupational and other roles necessary for adjustment. Since both types of change were substantial, applying the theorem that change induces change, they were likely to have important further results.

Changes in methods of production, as well as in transportation, underlay the great changes in everyday life. Both electric power and automotive transportation initially reduced the economies of scale in manufacturing and shipping. Steam engines are more efficient as size increases, whereas an electric motor running a single hand-tool has very nearly the same efficiency as the biggest power installation. This helped to keep small-scale manufacturing alive and also made for higher productivity from industrial capital following World War I.[1] In addition the wide geographical spread of reasonably high priced electric power freed plants from the need for being located where they had access to cheap coal. Since less than carload lots were expensive to handle for both railroads and shippers, the small producer could not compete with the large if rail transportation was a significant factor in cost. The motor-truck, however, could efficiently fit each scale of needs and, all factors considered, undersell the railroad on short haul freight of any kind.

To these new freedoms in industrial size and location the passenger automobile added an expansion of the local labour market to a thirty- to forty-mile radius and made possible the location of many types of business activity in urban fringe areas. Slow development of efficient rural trucks in the twenties and during the depression checked the impact of this great complex of social change until World War II. Starting with the building of war plants in places that could tap under-employed rural

[1] As will be brought out in the next chapter, smaller proprietary businessmen play very different roles in business, politics and society from those of corporate bureaucrats. In preserving this group in manufacturing and shipping, the dual revolution was in reality preserving past roles and attitudes, rather than accelerating change.

labour, there was an 'urban explosion' that brought within thirty years a redistribution of United States population which more than doubled the proportion living near, but not in, cities. The aeroplane also added to the decentralizing effects of electricity and motor vehicles, leading to more operations in dispersed small plants, now easily reached by executives from the head office.

By 1970 nearly 40 per cent of the population of the United States lived in what the census classed as the suburban parts of 'metropolitan' areas, and all but a small fraction of 'rural' people were in close contact with cities. This meant a majority facing the new or accentuated problems of adjusting to rapidly changing roles and artificially created communities, where the status ladder was obvious on the basis of neighbourhood, house, automobiles, and clubs. The most prestigious and influential of the role-sets in the more prosperous of these suburbs were strongly devoted to preserving the status quo by strict definitions of role behaviour, difficult or impossible to achieve by those of somewhat lower economic status. Since geographical mobility was unusually high in these areas, neighbours and other associates in the growing communities offered the individual less of the inward reinforcement that had come from role-sets made up of old friends or even familiar acquaintances.

The long-run psychological effects of the freedom of personal movement brought about by the motor-car were still in the limbo of psychological testing. Every mature citizen, save for some central urban groups, was now a knight in armour who sallied forth, wrapped in one or two tons of steel, in whatever direction he pleased. Village stores and local services died from neglect by these knights of the road who could trade more effectively and find more amusement in larger centres. But this again meant the substitution of diffuse impersonal role-sets for ones made up of familiar people. The very act of going forth, while not as venturesome as that of a knight in Sherwood Forest, involved risks and nervous tensions that some commuters endured for two or more hours each day.

High geographical mobility, suburban living, and the nervous strains of movement by private cars combined to make a more tense, restless population with shallow roots 'who picked up and dropped friends the way they traded cars and houses'.[1] Such people, with weakly internalized roles, were susceptible to easy manipulation and ready changes in attitude in direations not contrary to the sanctions of existing institutions.[2] They still shared, that is, in the historic middle-class regard for property and fear of disruptive forces, such as invasion of their community by new ethnic groups, or loss of status through occupational change.

In addition, conservative influences were no doubt reinforced by the more or less conscious efforts of the sponsors of mass media to build a stable, uniform national community of high consumers, to reinforce 'the American way of life'. Whether better levels of education, made possible partly by the school bus, broader contacts through greater freedom of movement, and readily accessible varieties of aesthetically inspiring recreation, would overcome some of the traditional bourgeois attitudes remained a question. As noted in Chapter III, Professor Marcuse thought this new leisure-time culture was designed by big business to preserve 'surplus repression', or the *status quo*.

In spite of its importance to suburban America the greatest impact of the dual revolution before 1970 was on farm life. The new technology had the most profound social and economic effects of any change in agricultural history. Here, as in decentralization, there was a damming-up and bursting-out effect coupled with World War II. While, on the historic basis of specialization in wheat, corn, cotton, and meat for both home consumption and export, the third of the nation who were then farmers had prospered from the beginning of the century to the collapse of 1920, for the next twenty years they faced economic difficulties. Unusual demand for wheat and cotton in World War

[1] H. L. Wilensky: 'Work, Careers and Social Integration', in Tom Burns, ed., *Industrial Man: Selected Readings* (Baltimore: Penguin, 1969), p. 129.

[2] When David Riesman writes of 'other directed People' he does not mean primarily pragmatists or opportunists, but rather people who readily accepted new role directions from outside sources.

I, and easily secured government and local bank loans, had over-expanded production in all staple crops, and brought into cultivation marginal lands not needed when world trade returned to normal. In addition, motorized equipment was replacing horses, mules, and oxen that fed on some of the staples. These causes brought financial troubles that were made somewhat worse by movements toward agricultural self-sufficiency in Europe, and disastrously worse by the Great Depression.

The effect of the relief measures of the New Deal was to keep owners on their farms by subsidies for acreage restriction, and also to put some of the poor on new farms. While the secular trend was already toward fewer farms, these government policies slightly increased the number, so that from 1910 to 1940 the total remained slightly above 6 million, and at the latter date about a quarter of the population of the United States still lived on farms, but the 'agricultural adjustment' programmes failed to bring back farm prosperity.

In these twenty years of low profits or actual losses, few farmers or other interests were tempted to invest capital in agriculture, and few young men of ability chose farming as an occupation. As a result, specialized petrol-powered machines, new knowledge of soil biology and chemistry, hybrid seeds for grain, ways to increase yields of milk, eggs, and meat by breeding all accumulated without being put into general use.

When World War II suddenly produced excess demand, the dam burst and all the stored-up knowledge of methods, materials and specialized machines came into use. The result was an upsurge in agricultural productivity which, in turn, greatly altered the life patterns of farmers. In 1970 rapid change was still going on. Statistics present amazing contrasts—such, for example, as a 150 per cent increase in productivity per man-hour on farms from 1950 to 1966 as compared with less than half that much in manufacturing. The true extent of the difference, however, is concealed by the fact that, for a majority of small cultivators, farming still existed as a way of life rather than of maximizing income. In 1965, out of over three million farms, 750,000 provided nine-tenths of the product. Surely a million farms manned by less than two million owners or full-time workers, in 1970, could have supplied all of the necessary product. This figure would about equal that for employment in 'transportation equipment'. In size, also, an increase in the average farm from 167 acres in 1940 to above 400 acres in 1970 did not show the true economic situation. Many listed by the census as 'commercial' farms, those selling at least $2,500 worth of product annually, were in fact part-time operations of families with members commuting to others jobs. Depending upon the type of crop, the farms responsible for all but 10 per cent of the product might run from 500 to thousands of acres, and be owned by corporations contracting with, or subsidiaries of, the food-processing firms.

Even on the smaller farms ways of life preserved for centuries changed in a generation. In 1930 only a negligible percentage of farms had electricity, tractors, trucks or radio, and, of course, none had television. In 1970 practically every commercial farm had all of these, plus an immense amount of specialized machinery not on the market at the earlier date. Even moderately successful farming had become a capital-intensive industry, controlled by college-educated agricultural experts, who probably used and needed more specialized knowledge than the small manufacturer or distributor.

Since the 1950s, agricultural sociologists have not seen any marked distinction between the social characteristics of the commercial farmer and those of the industrial employee living on the urban fringe. There were still, however, rural areas remote from large cities, such as those in the plains states, where the farmer's role and his role-set differed significantly from those of workers drawing their incomes chiefly from industry. While automotive and electronic devices have put even the remote farmers in touch with cities and the great 'community' of the mass media, people working only on their own farms were not subject to the same status pressures and psychological strains as suburbanites. The very fact of security in relations with their major role-sets tended to make them contented with things as they had been and likely to resist the threat of too great an invasion of urban or world ideas. Hence, like suburbanites, but for different reasons, they could form a reactionary type of resistance to social changes as such.[1]

In their effect on the sectors of the society that by 1970 were 95 per cent of the whole, increases of industrial efficiency and variety were more important than those in agriculture. Up to 1965, the greatest rise in productivity per man-hour in industry for any decade of the century came during the 1920s, not so much from scientific management or the mechanized assembly line as from the application of electricity, chemistry, and quality controls to industrial processes, while railroads and trucks also helped by substantial improvements in the efficiency of transportation. The sharp upswing in the 1920s contrasts with the slower gain in productivity during the period 1950 to 1965, when so-called automation was first being applied to plants and offices.

Reasons for this paradox are numerous, and like most paradoxes it conceals a contrary truth; the chief device of the new automation was the digital computer, a machine only invented at the close of World War II and not perfected for commercial purposes until the 1950s. It scarcely need be said that it was a very expensive and complicated aid, hard to apply to actual production routines, and undergoing technical change at a rate that outmoded costly quipment within a few years. In office procedures the computere permitted marked efficiencies in management, through allowing, for example, different types of accounting to be applied simultaneously, exact inventory control, and better forecasting and decisions in cases where many measurable factors were involved. But by 1970 it was only beginning to reduce substantially the numbers employed in either the managerial or clerical ranks. Programming and feeding a computer was a labour-consuming task that required both highly skilled and semi-skilled workers.

[1] Suburbanites suffered from trying to maintain material status in a continually changing human environment which led to fear of disruptive change. Farmers in contrast felt secure in their familiar environment and so also were resistant to change. Or more generally, role-players and role-sets usually welcome change only in certain limited directions that reinforce internalized sanctions.

As a result, the efforts of medium-sized firms with much paper work, such as brokerage houses of all types, to introduce computers may well have caused very substantial losses between 1960 and 1970.

In plants easily susceptible to automation by older devices the process had already progressed so far by the mid-fifties that the computers of that 'generation' could not immediately do much more; they could not, for example, efficiently load and drive a truck or make many minor adjustments that depended on judgment and manual dexterity. But with the rate of improvement in computer systems that had been achieved by 1970, basic economic, social and probably political changes seemed only a matter of time.

As we have seen, television was also still too new in 1970 for sound generalizations regarding its long-run effect on social change. In office use it was closely allied to computer systems that would project categories of material on cathode-ray screens, of which any items could be retrieved in greater detail by pointing at the required part with an electrically lit 'pencil'.[1]

An indirect but profoundly important result of the revolutions in technology was a growing belief that the society was affluent and poverty could and should be eliminated. Until the 1930s at least, poverty had been regarded as a proper penalty for laziness and vice, it had the aura of sin. Now the affluent, while probably still blaming the poor for their plight, saw poverty, aggravated by racial inequality, as a menace to an orderly society, that should be ended by some government action. It seems probable that no substantial segment of any middle class had earlier seen the economy as strong enough, if education and work were properly organized, to give relative comfort to all. While this new affluence was common to much of the western world, real family incomes were highest in the United States, and alleviation of distress could most easily be borne economically. Yet divisions between state and federal government and contrary political

[1] See Roger Meetham, *Information Retrieval: The Essential Technology*, London: Aldus Books, 1969, pp. 148–53.

traditions made action difficult. Change was obviously under way, but by 1970 its course was not clear.

Turning from the external effects of technology to those on the social roles of men on the job in the new types of industry, called for convenience work roles, the changes up to 1970 were somewhat contradictory. Motor vehicles emphasized the 'large batch', assembly-line type of production with many workers under one supervisor. This was thought by specialists in industrial relations to produce the least satisfactory work roles and the most labour trouble.[1] The production of electrical equipment itself had many of the same characteristics, but the application of electricity in industry both preserved smaller plants with single-unit production methods and made possible more continuous flow and automated technology, usually referred to as the 'process' type of production. In both of these forms work roles were generally either more varied or less demanding. In a few new highly automated companies where labour costs were generally low, all workers were put on salaries and might expect gradual advancement. By the late 1960s, industrial sociologists were coming to regard daily wages as inappropriate in a modern economy.[2]

In all types of large-scale factory production, increasingly good machinery, some attention to the comfort and morale of the workers, a shortening of work hours from an average of 60 per week in 1900 to under 40 by 1970, and a gradual substitution of knowledge for physical energy tended to make work roles increasingly less onerous than in the nineteenth century. Scolars of industrial relations were inclined to think that the worst period of labour unrest, as distinct from the normal pressure for higher wages and fringe benefits, have passed.[3] In any case, in 1970 all blue-collar factory roles involves only a fifth of the labour force, and assembly-line workers only a small part of this group.

[1] J. Woodward, 'Management and Technology', in Burns, *Industrial Man,* p. 211.

[2] A. L. Stinchcombe, 'Social Structure and the Invention of Organizational Forms', in Burns, *Industrial Man,* p. 183.

[3] Clark Kerr, John T. Dunlop, Frederick H. Harbison and Charles A. Myers, Industrialism and Industrial Man (London: Oxford University Press, 1964, p. 184).

After about 1930 the immediate contribution of the dual revolution to changes in the total of work roles, therefore, had been moderate. But by 1970 the combined effect of all the changes discussed so far, including more education, more lifelong exposure to electronic mass media, more automated processes in manufacturing and services, and fewer manual assembly lines and skilled hand trades, seemed destined to be great during the next generation.

It also appeared likely that the work roles of middle management, technicians and professionals would be affected as much as those of the lower levels. Whole ranks of middle management, both line and staff, might be eliminated by computers, and these men might not readily find new employment at equally good jobs. Such painful changes in status would affect many people who were likely to be influence-welding members of middle-class role-sets. As the process of change appeared to be accelerating the new roles called for would probably continue to be as remote from the older ones as those that caused 'the generation gap' of the 1960s.

The more exacting or intolerant role-sets of suburban life, an indirect effect of the Dual Revolution, may have been more important in controlling social change than were alterations in conditions of work. As noted earlier, the major directions of change from the new role and role-set relations were still not clear in 1970. But methods of adjustment and reconciliation in both occupational and community life might well (would almost have to) improve if the society was to avoid types of disruptive change unwanted by the majority.[1]

[1] There is a great difference between role changes that merely involve new mechanical behaviour and those that call for new internalized values or normative sanctions. Tensions would arise, for example, not from the difficulty of handling new technology, but from the real or feared changes in social status involved.

CHAPTER VII

PROPRIETARY AND MANAGERIAL
ENTERPRISE

One of the major institutions created by the sum-total of industrial technology was the big business corporation. Necessitated first by the increasing division of labour and scale of machinery, the corporation ultimately outgrew its technological origins and became an institution for controlling capital and markets. By this time the roles and sanctions governing the behaviour of the corporation as an entity were patterned by the needs for effective playing of roles in bureaucratic organizations.

This quick tropical growth to giantism at the end of the nineteenth century made its controllers the most conspicuous businessmen. They were the men most often quoted in the daily papers, the ones who sat on boards to advise the President or were called upon to staff his Cabinet. These chief executive employees of the largest corporations were, however, a small but precocious offshoot of the total world of business. The actual owners and proprietors of enterprise have not been an organized or homogeneous group, and although they have given the United States a businesslike culture, it has not been through the deliberate use of power, politically or socially, but rather through emulation of their roles in the adoption by others of their everyday habits and customs.

Thus, while it is necessary to interpret American history in terms of the influence of 'business', this force is a complex of many different types of folkways, mores, values and methods. On some political issues such as labour legislation, business has usually presented a united front; on others, such as tariffs or subsidies, it has fragmented. In order to discuss these multiple pressures on social change it is necessary first to survey the business population.

Examination of firms by size and activity, in 1970, showed almost every form of business that had ever existed historically from pack-peddlers to supermarket chains, and from family enterprises in a single home to corporations with hundreds of thousands of employees. On the whole, the characteristics of management would form the most meaningful social indexes, but they are unfortunately ones not carried in the census. The available ways to analyse business structure are by number of firms, employees per firm, or value added to the product.

From 1900 to 1970 the total number of firms grew much faster than the human population. This figure, however, included many businesses created solely for tax purposes, whose proprietors were chiefly engaged in some other activity, and hence the very high total is rather meaningless. A more reliable index of the increase in enterprises is the number of firms employing at least one worker, which since the late 1930s has been carefully checked by the Social Security Administration. In 1965 there were three and a half million such non-agricultural firms, two-thirds of which had less than four employees. A trend that surprises many scholars not familiar with the situation is that in total numbers small and medium-sized firms were increasing much more rapidly than large. From 1945 to 1965 the number of companies employing over 500 workers increased 50 per cent while every smaller category more than doubled. Meanwhile, population had risen by less than half. If one turns to percentage of the total labour force employed by firms with over 500 workers the same trends emerge; the big firms employed more than a quarter of the labour force in 1945 and less than that portion in 1965.

Looking at the number of enterprises from the standpoint of type of activity, retail trade has always had by far the most firms, making up nearly half of the total. Service of all types has come next, and manufacturing has only accounted for about one-tenth of the total. Hence, if we think of business decision-makers in point of numbers the small trade and service people have always been in the majority. In contrast to these millions of proprietors the mere thousands of executives who make policy in the big corporations are a small minority.

If, instead of numbers of policy-making managers, the business scene is viewed from the standpoint of production of goods and services the picture has been somewhat different, but even here it has been easy to over-emphasize the importance of the big enterprises whose names are household words. Aside from finance, which involves difficulty in making comparisons, most of the big companies were in public utilities, transportation and manufacturing. Using value added to the product as a measure, a long-range pattern of considerable stability in the relations of big firms to smaller ones in manufacturing emerged. Alfred D. Chandler, Jr., has recorded the percentage of such total value arising from industries with a high degree of monopoly or oligopoly (defined as six companies or less producing half, or twelve or less than three-quarters of the industry's total). He finds the percentages to have been 16 in 1909, 21 in 1929, 28 in 1939, and a variation from 26 to 28 between then and his final figure of 27 per cent in 1963. In other words, big company influence in markets rose from 1909 to 1939 and from then on has levelled off. In explanation of this stability the anti-trust division of the Department of Justice has been an important factor.

In maturing industrial nations, service industries in which small enterprises predominated grew more rapidly in number and employees than manufacturing. If the United States, since 1950, had not been spending up to 10 per cent of its gross national product on military operations and equipment, which emphasized industrial production, the shift to service would, of course, have been more pronounced. Furthermore, big industry has been able and probably will continue to eliminate labour by automation more rapidly than smaller-scale manufacturing, transportation, trade, or service. This leads to the startling but logical conclusion that in the future more men should be working for smaller employers, most of whom will be in trade and service. It also means that the managerial élite should become more diffuse, stemming from more firms and activities, rather than concentrated in 500 or 1000 big companies.

American businessmen, on the whole, have given scant attention to means of wielding personal social or political power. As participants in society their roles have varied greatly with their type of activity. A major difference has been between the role of the man who deals only with employees or other businessmen and the one who has to meet retail customers. The latter, illustrated by managers or proprietors in finance, trade, and service, particularly some types of brokerage, have had to pay careful attention to detecting positive or negative sanctions from this all-important part of their role-set. Since success depended largely on making friends and providing efficient but largely routine service, the social roles tended to be static. Yet, because of the potential cash value of friends, men whose personality made them successful in such pursuits were usually more active in social and civic affairs than were those engrossed in the improvement of processes and the administration of change.

A result of this situation was that the businessmen likely to be most active in community affairs were those with static occupational roles, whose desires to win friends made it seem wise to behave in ways that reinforced the existing social norms. Meanwhile, the men used to innovation stuck to their last and took less part in outside social activities. The big corporation also exercised a confining influence by consuming so much of the time and energy of administrators, and moving younger ones so frequently from one locality to another, that they tended to pay little attention to politics or civic affairs. The role-sets that mattered most to them were company colleagues or their own families. Hence, as careerism in management, technology or professional advising continues to grow, the business influence in state and local politics, left to proprietors of retail trade and service establishments, may become more right-wing Republican.

In considering social change as a whole, the influence of all business executives was likely to be conservative. Even if they played innovative roles in their work, and adjusted readily to ensuing change, they would either sooner have external relations remain constant and predictable, or else they were simply not interested, and went along readily with trade and service groups which opposed change. Any businessmen active in civic and political affairs were likely to be those who had acquired good incomes and could leave work routines safely in the hands of younger people. This not only made them conservative because of advancing age, but also fearful of potential changes with which the people they had left in charge could not cope.

While in local and state affairs the representatives of certain medium-sized businesses, plus politically oriented lawyers, were likely to be the most active, in national affairs this group could generally exert conservative influence only through their congressmen or politically weak trade associations. In contrast the top executives of the big corporations could, if they chose, use the money and personnel of a great organization to influence political or social affairs. Consideration of the degree to which they were likely to do this, and their relationship to social change within business itself, requires an examination of the internal demands and politics of corporate bureaucracies.

In the early twentieth century the executives of big business, more than those in state or federal governments, studied and developed rules for the administration of bureaucratic systems. In the first decade of the century alone, 240 books on the 'science' of management were published. While no bureaucracy could escape certain problems, in business administrative control or power has been more centralized and easier to wield; hence, theoretically at least, business could solve problems more efficiently than government.

In reality, business corporations had more highly centralized power than the early law-makers had intended. In state charters, which had reached a fair degree of uniformity by 1900, the stockholders, voting on the basis of the shares owned by each, elected a board of directors usually for limited terms, and this board hired the necessary employees and ran the company. But, in fact, from the earliest days of big companies in the 1830s, the system had never worked this way. The stockholders of large corporations, scattered all over the nation, were unwilling to assume the expense of attending the annual meeting. Management solicited proxies and voted the stock of the small investor. While the directors had legal power over management, unless they were officers of the company as well, they lacked the knowledge of the affairs of the organization necessary for wise decisions. The result was that even by 1900 largely self-perpetuating hired managers, not the owning capitalists, ran the big companies, and within the top group one man generally exercised final authority.

The major limitation imposed by directors representing capital ownership came in decisions requiring large-scale financing. In such instances important capitalists or representatives of invest-ment banking houses on the board might have the final say. There were also some companies in which a family owned enough of the stock to control elections, as with Ford or DuPont, but by World War I such instances were rare. While family control of large companies has steadily diminished, ultimate sovereignty by outside financial interests has waxed and waned depending on a number of legal, market and tax factors that need not be examined here. The rise of conglomerate holding com-panies in the sixties was a new assertion of the power of the mas-ters of finance over individual company management, but, as the troubles of some conglomerates illustrated, it was not easy for outsiders to make efficient decisions for a corporate bureaucracy.

Since each type of production, marketing and service led to different forms of management it was hard to find universal principles. Study in the 1950s of a sample of one hundred British manufacturing plants of various sizes and types developed no close correlation between adhering to the most advanced theories of management and commercial success.[1] It appeared that

[1] J. Woodward, in Burns, *Industrial Man*, p. 196. This generalization might not apply to a hundred or more giant companies in the United States, which have highly structured systems. See Alfred D. Chandler, Jr., *Strategy and Structure: Chapters in the History of American Industrial Enterprise*, Cambridge, Mass., M.I.T. Press, 1962.

successful performance of managerial roles depended more on the motivation and total personality of the actor than on any fixed or scientific rules. While there were, of course, elementary principles such as respect for channels of authority and clearly understood delegation of power, on the level of over-all successful coordination management appeared more an art than a science. As a consequence of this variability comprehensive understanding of the implications of the managerial, as distinct from the proprietary, role developed slowly.

Study of the evolving role may begin with noting how men properly qualified as managerial artists were conditioned while struggling to reach the top, and this, in turn, involves some of the problems of bureaucracy. The qualities needed to get ahead in the organization were loyalty, unquestioning acceptance of hard work, good judgment, outward adherence to the social norms, a friendly, genial but decisive personality, and in a really big corporation some luck in becoming visible in a favourable light to men higher up. Speaking for publication, executives were prone to emphasize one or another of the earlier qualities of this list. David Sarnoff as president of the Radio Corporation of America in the 1950s said: 'The most important factor in determining whether a man is a really satisfactory employee . . . is . . . his family life. If he has a *normal* happy family life, a good home, he is a satisfactory *normal* fellow.'[1] At about the same time C. H. Buford, a railroad president, advised an aspiring young man to 'cultivate and develop a pleasing personality . . . show an interest in other people and what they have to say'.[2] William Stephen of Goodyear said the same thing in a different way: 'We can't consider a man for promotion unless he has built a smooth running organization.'[3]

Such admonitions indicated how cautious the player of administrative roles in big companies had to be in divining the positive sanctions of the most important members of his role-set,

[1] Eugene Staley, ed. *Creating an Industrial Civilization*, New York: Harper, 1952, p. 62.
[2] 'How to Become a Railroad President', *What's New* (November 1949), p. 13.
[3] Quoted in Paul W. Litchfield, *Industrial Voyage*, Garden City: Doubleday, 1954, p. 130.

while at the same time trying to avoid strong adverse sanctions from those of less influence. This type of role-playing was called 'other directed' by David Riesman, and the personality produced was labelled 'the organization man' by William Whyte. In few other areas does the model of roles, role-sets and accepted institutions function as clearly as in the long career ladder of the big corporation.[1]

A major problem of bureaucracies was that the qualities that would bring a man to the top and the attitudes they engendered were not, from the standpoint of the stockholders, necessarily most desirable in a chief executive. These qualities could lead to over-emphasis on satisfying the members of the bureaucracy at the expense of innovation and assumption of reasonable economic risks.

The logical motivation for men at the top was not profit as such; often they were not large stockholders in the company, but rather the long-run welfare of the organization, that would guarantee good salaries and pensions. Such emphasis on security was creating the 'welfare corporation' in the welfare state. With unusual candour, Frank Abrams, as Chairman of Standard Oil of New Jersey, said: 'Modern management might well measure its success or failure as a profession in large part by the satisfaction it is able to produce for its employees.'[2] Part of such satisfaction among the salaried employees would be the assurance for the future given by maintenance of the company's position relative to its competitors in the market. After World War II this became a more popular measure among corporate leaders than absolute rates of profit. It could mean that, if all companies made the same mistake, the only ones to suffer would be the consumers, or possibly the stockholders.

Another way of looking at the influences affecting the playing of the chief executive role could be based on the principle of satisfying the role-sets in their order of importance. In such a hierarchy fellow executives and perhaps one or two influential

---

[1] Hence the lack of explanatory footnotes in this chapter.

[2] Herryman Maurer, *Great Enterprise: Growth and Behaviour of the Big Corporation*, New York: Macmillan, 1955, p. 161.

directors would probably rank first, employees in general next, and the mass of stockholders who were never seen last. Satisfying customers was of course a long-run essential, but this usually depended more on specialized advice than on the way in which the executive played his role. Since these precepts based on long-run security violated the expressed doctrines of nineteenth-century capitalism, this view of the role was acknowledged only gradually by those who played it. While advanced managers in the 1920s, such as Walter Gifford of the Telephone Company, talked of the long view of corporate management and of the stockholders as an important asset for public relations, and Edward Filene and others stressed duty toward employees, most men continued to talk the traditional language of profit for the stockholders as the chief sanction bearing upon the executive role.

But ambiguity in aims at the top was only one of the troubles of bureaucratic organizations. Each young college graduate starting, hopefully, on an upward career was soon conscious of contradictory motives. Loyalty to the corporation was a *sine qua non*, and this required selfless cooperation for the welfare of the group, while at the same time each member was in keen competition with the rest for promotion. Such a situation, of course, generated political moves and alliances both inside and outside the particular department, which might well interfere with the supposed primary aim of efficient production.

Continuing what may be called the pathology of bureaucracy, common features were that organizations were relatively easy to build up (because nearly everyone was moving ahead), followed the form or structure common to their type of activity in the period of their origin, and then became resistant to later change. The sociologist Tom Burns notes three strategies that men in established bureaucracies used to ward off or delay adjusting to change: first, they might pass the matter on to a superior who could, in turn, do the same thing, so that all matters ultimately reached the president, who might be too busy to give his attention to a complex proposal; second, a decision could be put off by appointing a committee to deliberate on the need for action; or third, the challenge could be met by the creation of a new department, with additional jobs, whose future growth would logically depend upon enlargement of the problem.[1]

Continuing dedication to the aims of the company was also a problem. No matter how flexible and well run a big bureaucratic structure was, most of its middle managers, those who neither initiated nor physically executed policy, necessarily failed to achieve one of the limited number of high posts. This may explain why David McClelland, about 1960, found government managers ranking ahead of private in their achievement motivation score, and found the highest motivation among the young managers who, presumably, still had hope.[2] The middle-aged man who knew he was stuck compensated in various ways. He might build his life and ambitions more around goals outside the company, such as leadership in his community, excelling at a sport, or professional achievement. Within the company he might take refuge in extreme specialization, often referred to as 'technicism'. If in his specialty he became recognized as an authority, this also could bring compensation through outside prestige. Obviously, such compensation was far easier for a staff officer, who was by training a specialist, than for a line officer who had risen from the less educated ranks.

Partly because of differences in education, social status, and age, and perhaps also because of the practical man's fear of displacement by the technicians of knowledge, there was usually friction between staff and line. By the 1960s staff people were nearly all college-educated, and usually interested in outside professional recognition. The sociologist Wilbert E. Moore has called them the 'two-faced experts', who had loyalties divided between the company and their professional discipline. Many experienced chief executives held that these highly educated specialists, as well as some of the rest of middle management, were not at this stage of their careers businessmen in the traditional meaning of the word.

[1] Burns, *Industrial Man*, pp. 244–7.
[2] 'Business Drive and National Achievement', in Etzionis, *Social Change*, p. 169.

It was irksome for middle-aged line officers dependent on long experience to be told what to do by young men with doctorates from socially prestigious universities, and, as a result, there was considerable opposition to staff suggestions for internal change. The clever staff man who wanted to get ahead learned the political arts of compromise, some of which, such as secretly sharing some of a big R-D budget with a line department, while not corrupt in the sense of illicit private gain, nevertheless tended to give top management a distorted idea of what was taking place.

One device used by big companies with many plants partly to resist the growth of bureaucratic habits was to move the ablest young men from place to place every three or four years. Although the expressed aim was to acquaint the rising man with the practices and problems of all the branches, continuous movement gave them the experience of playing their administrative roles with various role-sets, perhaps stimulating new ideas, while attaching men to the company as their only permanent community. Service in foreign branches or subsidiaries were expansions of the same system which also brought new, and sometimes troublesome, ideas back to the home office.

Offsetting their essentially political and sociological internal problems, large corporations had some efficiencies not available within smaller enterprises. They could have staff experts bringing all available knowledge to bear on research and decisions. Because of the scale of operations, they could more efficiently use computers and other costly forms of automation. Since they usually shared markets with only a few competitors they could gear buying, production and prices to business cycle forecasts on the basis that their relative competitive positions would not suddenly change. This latter ability was a protection for the corporation against excessive inventory in either raw materials or finished goods, but externally such policy would tend to accentuate both upswings and downswings of the business cycle.

Smaller firms might have the benefit from most of these economies by hiring experts from outside consultants, and in some cases this might result in lower proportionate overhead, but the smaller competitor could not raise prices or forecast sales as readily as the semi-monopolistic corporation. In the late 1950s, as foreign investment came to seem more desirable than more rapid domestic expansion, the big firm also had an advantage, although not one that could not be overcome by cooperation between smaller native and foreign entrepreneurs.

It should be clear from all the preceding discussion that corporate managers were generally preoccupied with goals other than national political or social power. Yet, in spite of this and their small numbers in relation to other types of businessmen, in the eyes of many people, including scholars and foreigners, they typified both business and its influence in the United States. In a pluralistic society there were, to be sure, sound reasons for assigning the most important managers a large share of potential influence. They had access to the specialized knowledge of their staffs and could be supplied with speeches and articles for any occasion. The staff men in public relations carefully built the image of the company and its executives, and advised them regarding grants for education, politics, or public welfare. The big company could afford lobbyists and 'contract' men at state and national levels, while their chief executives served on national commissions and committees and might become personal friends of presidents.

In practice, however, the top managers, seldom united on aims, were not a ruling or political power élite. While many big companies wanted military contracts, and from 1939 on found it wise to have representatives of the military in their employ, and contract men in Washington, this was a specialized and usually unstable department of the company. The middle-class careerists who ultimately reached the top of big corporations normally had neither the continuous interest nor the right qualities for personally playing political roles in a democratic government. They preferred to support mass media and professional politicians who would wield the actual power, and in such a very large nation the support of any one company was not likely to bind a major politician. Politicians were probably influenced as much by their own, personal business interests as by money or other pressures from constituents. Pluralism, or the Galbraithian idea of counter-vailing powers, appeared to have operated, with the qualification that the business élite had better access than other groups to the most important men in politics and the professions, and could more easily conceal small favours in large expense accounts, but such efforts were usually for the welfare of the company, not the individual executive.

The older business attitudes of wanting freedom to make revolutionary changes in technology, while having society and its politics go on as before, persisted among the managerial élite. In their internal affairs managers used sanctions in terms of 'judicial' or 'objective' attitudes, but in external relations they tended to resist impending change on the basis of the demands of the market or the needs of the economy. Big business con-tinued to be in the ambiguous but historic position of encouraging change through large expenditures for research and development, while opposing social change resulting from new technology through support of conservative politicians.

The rise of big organizations, therefore, was responsible for economic rather than substantial political changes in the nature of capitalism. One important economic change arose from the ability of the semi-monopolistic companies to 'administer' prices to fit costs. This, coupled with the importance of good morale within the company, produced managerial attitudes in labour relations quite different from those of proprietors. Since the workers as fellow employees were part of the company, and their cooperation was important for good uninterrupted production, there was a built-in element of inflation in wage bargaining. These companies sold in markets in which small increases in price by all firms might have little effect on the volume of sales. Certainly as between a prolonged and bitter labour conflict and a somewhat inflationary wage increase the latter was preferable. Only in times when the market was poor, as in 1970, would the managerial élite risk a prolonged strike over the question of wages. Smaller employers were in a weaker position in relation to national unions and generally had to agree to similar advances. Thus the rates established by union bargaining in the big companies and subsequent price increases also gave a continuous upward trend to white-collar salaries and wages throughout business.

This situation produced a political paradox. The companies faced with the largest wage demands feared the growth of government power more than they feared inflation. Consequently they generally opposed wage-price guide lines and compulsory mediation. The workers, who usually had political attitudes different from those of management, nevertheless agreed with them on this point. As a result, neither conservative nor liberal politicians wanted to take a stand in favour of what had come to be known as incomes policy.

Another important change came from evolving financial practices which struck at the central traditional mechanism of capitalism: individual risk-taking investment. As high income taxes cut the rate of saving of many of the old rich and the prosperous professional and managerial groups, higher real wages and salaries allowed more saving at the middle income levels. While these 'little' people did not form a workable commercial market for the sale of new securities of a single company, cautious small investors would buy a few shares in a mutual fund. Such organizations, pension funds, insurance companies and the investments from trust estates and long extensions of credit by banks came to form the principal market for new capital. An analysis of new financing from 1957 to 1961 showed the sources to be: internal corporate saving 60 per cent; bank credits 20; funds of all types 15; and direct private investment a mere 5. By the 1960s there were some 25 million stockholders, including those in mutual funds, but they were unimportant as a direct source of new capital. Since the most important function of the old capitalist role was to supply capital, the economic system appeared to have moved to an institutional rather than an individual form of capitalism.

This transition was in tune with many of the roles of the managerial élite, such as their behaviour in ways favourable to corporate welfare and internal security rather than to maximization of current profit. Their role-sets, composed chiefly of other successful bureaucrats, of course approved. A few strong individual capitalists still fought, or tried to take advantage of the managerial attitudes. Some of these men, such as James Ling or Howard Hughes, employing the assets of one company to buy another, put large firms into conglomerate structures and dismissed many managers without regard to internal welfare or security in a given company. These operators were oriented toward profit from the manipulation of securities, or other financial means, and in the steadily rising market from 1960 to 1967 they appeared to be reintroducing an old and more ruthless phase of capitalism. But in the less prosperous years thereafter, the conglomerates did poorly. In general, the largest and probably most efficient companies were still on the outside as competitors, and new managers, selected because of supposed financial ability, often proved lacking in understanding of the internal problems of a particular company. To a degree, the troubles of these rapidly shifted chief executives demonstrated that there was still no reliable general science of management; that it continued to depend on specific knowledge and successful human relations.

By 1970 the managerial élite still seemed likely to play social roles guided more and more by internal institutional considerations, which might, of course, involve special external relations with government, labour, and the public. One could also foresee a 'technologizing' of business in the leading nations which, through a new world of specialized knowledge, would confuse most of the old distinctions in occupation and status. The difference between publicly and privately employed managers had already decreased, and, somewhat more gradually, the difference between public and privately institutionalized enterprise. Since these changes would affect the smaller businessmen much more slowly, the two parts of the business world seemed likely to move further apart ideologically, with the more active influences in state or local politics, at least, continuing to come from the more traditionally oriented proprietors.

CHAPTER VIII

DEMOGRAPHIC FORCES

Since where and how people live is one of the major forces in shaping institutions and roles, demography, or the study of population and its movement, is basic to social change. With a few exceptions, such as the creation of company towns, or transportation of some groups by government order or private contract, large movements were based on thousands or millions of individual decisions, difficult to analyse historically. In contrast, the over-all statistics of population change are tolerably well collected in the United States and have been extensively interpreted.

In the period from 1900 to 1914, for the first time since the early 1850s, population grew more from immigration than from domestic births. Since the immigrants were mainly adults of working age, whose upbringing and schooling had been paid for elsewhere, they increased the number of workers in relation to the dependent part of the population. Meanwhile, as natives migrated from country to city, domestic fertility rates declined, which also increased the ratio of producers to those under working age. The results of both factors were: nearly a 10 per cent increase in the proportion of the population in the productive labour force; and a growth in urban households which, in turn, raised consumer demands. These all had secondary effects that have not yet been fully studied. For example, it was probably easier for progressive reformers to restrict child labour and enact compulsory schooling by state laws than it would have been in a period of higher fertility and relative increase in young dependents.[1]

[1] This decade of a rapidly increasing percentage of employed workers and rising industrial productivity was nevertheless a period of inflation, showing the many factors bearing on price, notably in this case a demand for agricultural products that tended to exceed the supply, and increased military spending by the major powers, including the United States.

While economically immigration was the ideal way to increase the labour force, either skilled or unskilled, not only because the workers came free of expense for rearing and education, but also because the supply turned itself off in periods of unemployment, many citizens regarded this pre-war wave of immigrants as racially undesirable. Throughout the nineteenth century immigrants to the United States had come mainly from the United Kingdom, Germany, and Scandinavia. Although the Catholic Irish had caused initial resistance, on the whole these ethnic groups had been welcomed. By 1900, however, changes in the European pressures to emigrate had drastically altered the national origins of the immigrants who were arriving in unprecedented numbers, sometimes exceeding a million a year.

The 'new' immigration was composed chiefly of Jews from Russian Poland, various south-eastern minority groups from Austria-Hungary, and southern Italians. In general these people were short and dark-haired in contrast to the taller blond Germans and Scandinavians of the preceding period, or, as the amateur anthropologists of the day put it, the new group were Mediterranean rather than Nordic. A popular view among quite respectable social scientists was that only the Nordic 'races' had successfully developed and operated democratic institutions. In addition, Russian Jews were suspected of association with revolutionary movements, and Sicilian Italians with criminal organizations. Although the South, for example, was anxious to attract white workers, it wanted none of these types of immigrants.

Had northern manufacturers not profited from the influx of cheap labour, effective restriction might have come before World War I. Advocates of restriction such as the American Federation of Labor and numerous patriotic societies, picking on literacy tests as the most flexible and defensible means, helped to steer bills through Congress in 1912 and 1913, only to have them vetoed by Taft and Wilson respectively. While both Presidents argued that these laws violated the historic role of America as a haven for the oppressed, business interests wanted the vetoes. Finally in

1917, as a measure to satisfy labour in the war emergency, when immigration from Europe had practically ceased, Wilson agreed to a bill for a literacy test.

The Bolshevik Revolution and the post-war depression from 1920 to 1922 changed employer attitudes toward immigration. The middle and upper classes were scared that Leon Trotsky's prediction of world revolution might be fulfilled. With plenty of unemployed at home there seemed little reason for receiving potentially dangerous aliens. Between 1921 and 1929 a series of restrictions were imposed which ultimately provided quotas for each nation based on their contribution to the earlier population of the United States. This gave the United Kingdom, Germany, and the Scandinavian countries large quotas, drastically restricted the new types of immigrants and ruled out non-Caucasians. The total from all sources, except the nations of the Western Hemisphere, was set at a little over 150,000 a year, or less than 15 per cent of the numbers that seemed likely to have come under a free system.

From 1929 to 1945 depression and war made emigration from Europe, except to escape from German fascism, unimportant. After World War II, the 'National Origins Act' of 1929, with only minor modifications, continued to be the law, and as world population grew it now held back increasing hundreds of thousands who wished to come to the United States. An internal effect of continuing restriction was, of course, that the population became more native-born, and the once rigidly separated European ethnic groups began to be absorbed, but not at the rate predicted by earlier advocates of a melting-pot. As late as 1970 southern European family origin detracted from status, while religion and other differences, preserved partly to hold ethnic communities together, still proved barriers to intermarriage.

Unquestionably immigration produced strong forces both for and against social change. The new groups expanded the Catholic Church, previously dominated by the Irish, into an organization of many nationalities that became half as large as the total of all Protestant denominations. Increasing numbers of parochial schools conditioned children in the basically conservative attitudes of Catholicism. In eastern politics and labour movements Catholics were particularly influential. In the first three decades of the century, for example, a continuous majority of Catholics on the council of the American Federation of Labor aggressively resisted any official support for Eugene V. Debs and the rising socialists, or what might have become a labour party. The concentration of much of the new immigrant population in segregated parts of cities led ultimately to conservative resistance to a number of solutions for urban problems.[1]

The stimulating of change through introducing European ideas or 'high' culture was slight, because the immigrants were from the masses who had not progressed far in the educational systems of their homelands. They constituted a first generation, at least, wholly devoted to earning a living and establishing economic security for their families. The Jews, because of the intellectual character of their tenaciously preserved religious culture, were an exception. They introduced a respect for learning and the arts beyond that of old-stock natives of similar social status. The distinguished scientists and artists driven out of Germany by Hitler were, of course, in marked contrast to most earlier immigrants and became major instigators of progress.

Compared to the effects on social change of 350 years of migration within the United States, however, the great wave of immigration was a passing influence. The domestic migration most discussed historically was the gradual movement of farming from the East to the unsettled West, said by Frederic Jackson Turner to have most differentiated American from European institutions and to have virtually ended in 1890. While Turner was the first historian in the United States to lay stress on sociological rather than political or economic causation and is justly famed for initiating a revolution in American historiography, later scholars have found that, mainly, he was right for the wrong

[1] These instances show that strongly held values can produce conservative role-playing and role-sets, in spite of the tendency of migration to generate change. Domestically, however, demographers have found a correlation between areas of rapid in-migration and progressive political attitudes.

reasons, that he was an artist with a new insight, not an analytical social scientist.

Even the farming frontier failed to 'close' in 1890; no previous western land booms had equalled the Oklahoma, north-east Texas promotions of the first decade of the new century, and as a percentage of the total population the westward movement was about as great from 1900 to 1910 as from 1880 to 1890. In part, Turner's error was due to the fact that the westward movement had never been as much a product of free land or as heavily agricultural as his non-quantified hypothesis suggested. From 1862 to 1890 only a fifth of all new farms were titled under the Homestead Act, and trade, service, mining, timber, and transportation had all contributed heavily to the settlement of the West, often being the occupations of the men who first advanced into new regions. The movement of both agriculture and industry westward over the mountains to the Pacific coast was still continuing in 1970, when California became the most populous state.

In any case, the major volume of migration from 1850 on had not been to new land in the West, but from country to city and from one city to another. It was the continuing total of all forms of internal movement that differentiated the United States from more settled societies, and had perhaps always been the major force behind such 'American' characteristics as egalitarianism, activism and readiness to accept physical change.

In the mid-twentieth century the planned movement of promising young men by big business firms was matched by the voluntary movement of successful professionals of all types to take advantage of new opportunities. Demographers found that geographical mobility followed an 'S' curve, drawn with an X axis for income and a Y for movement, on which in the middle section the rate of migration increased with income until the highest levels were reached, where the peak of various careers bent the curve in an opposite direction. An élite in motion was certainly a major factor in novel role-playing and social change. It was part of the general pattern that justifies saying that, whereas the older nations adjusted industrialism to fit their society, the United States readjusted its people and customs to fit the demands of industrialism.

After 1914, with immigration no longer providing a large extra supply of labour for boom periods, the United States had to draw on both women and under-employed workers in rural areas. Female employees rose from 20 per cent of the total in 1920 to 35 per cent in 1965, and with office work increasing faster than plant or manual jobs the trend seemed likely to continue. The most visible group of under-employed in agriculture were the southern blacks, and, starting with the abrupt cutting off of European immigrants by World War I, negroes were encouraged to come north in large numbers. In each period of shortage of labour the process continued until by 1965 there were only 80,000 black sharecroppers left in the South, and, by 1970, in the nation as a whole, four-fifths of the negroes lived in cities. In drawing this vast black and white population to urban centres the principal employers involved not only entered into no plans for housing or welfare, but were opposed to the increased taxes that such plans would have required. While many such companies in fact controlled the governments of small cities, they held that their social responsibility ended at the pay window.[1]

The economist Richard A. Easterlin has pointed out the importance of the formation of new urban households in reinforcing major periods of prosperity and consequent changes in technology and social customs.[2] Each substantial upswing in business draws workers from the lower-wage rural or semi-rural to the higher-wage metropolitan areas, leading to formation of new households, with still more units added by the effect of prosperity in stimulating the urban marriage rate. The material needs of each new household, involving a tendency for about the first fifteen years to spend more than is received in income, reinforces and prolongs the period of high consumer demand.

[1] See Sidney Fine, *Sit-down: The General Motors Strike of 1936–1937*, Ann Arbor: University of Michigan Press, 1969, Ch. IV.

[2] *Population, Labour Force, and Long Swings in Economic Growth*, New York: Columbia Press for National Bureau of Economic Research, 1968, pp. 48–9.

Since urban households are permanently less self-sufficient than rural, the shift from farm households constituting 35 per cent of the total in 1900 to only 6 per cent in 1970 was a powerful long-run, but uneven, stimulant to changes caused by increasing market demand.

The economic effect of this rapid shift away from the manner in which most people had always lived prior to the nineteenth century affected all elements of the social system. Living in cities required new roles, altered older ones, formed new values, expanded learning, and changed the relation of most actors to their role-sets. Perhaps the shift from a predominantly rural to an urban society in the last hundred years in the United States is of more basic importance than all of the accompanying changes in technology.

The process of urbanization went through two phases: in the first, up to about 1910 or 1920, large densely built-up cities grew as production, marketing and information centres; the second phase, made possible by private motor-cars and rapid transit, was an expansion of these dense cores into sprawling metropolitan areas. The census calls a central city of over 50,000 and its thickly populated surrounding counties a 'standard metropolitan area'. On this basis 40 per cent of the population of the United States lived in such areas in 1930, and roughly 70 per cent in 1970. There were significant distinctions among the 200 or so metropolitan areas. About a dozen had most of the head offices of the nation-wide corporations, the banking facilities needed for large-scale finance, and a labour force with enough diversity in special skills to staff any type of activity. The remaining 200 were either supported by branch plants, regional distribution of national products, or locally owned special types of production. Those dependent on the branch plants of big companies have been called satellite cities, and until the end of World War II, at least, their civic life usually suffered from lack of local control of their main economic resources.

The traditional social learning and values of the United States were particularly unsuited to the problems of growth of the industrial city. The American ideal of a limited government, with a division of powers, inactively watching over a self-regulating economy with conflicts determined on the basis of competition in the market, was not a workable arrangement for the rapidly expanding urban centre. As Lewis Mumford pointed out, an unplanned city grew by progressively destroying itself. Areas originally built for housing were invaded by expanding industry, middle-class single-family dwellings were converted into multi-family tenements with no increase in sanitary facilities, while upper-class families abandoned the city as unfit for decent living. Their erstwhile mansions became offices for the service trades or merely disintegrated until replaced by an office building or apartment house. In the older parts of the big cities ghettos settled by particular ethnic groups clung to their locations regardless of the encroachments of objectionable plants such as slaughter-houses or chemical works. The old downtown streets adequate for an age that depended on public transportation soon proved entirely inadequate for automobiles, trucks and parking. Two-lane bridges, once proud architectural monuments, became unavoidable bottlenecks for traffic. Wrap this expensively non-functional jumble of archaic parts in a smog of coal smoke and petroleum vapour, and one has the industrial city as it had developed by the 1930s.

Early attempts at urban improvement, precursors of the more general progressive movement, were directed, not at over-all planning, but at improving the efficiency of government and alleviating the living conditions of the poor. The great deluge of immigrants flooding the cities from 1898 on made both of these problems rapidly worse. Even in earlier decades city politicians had found their strongest support in the slum wards, with their more numerous voters. In the days before American governments supplied desperately needed services, the ward leaders held the support of the poor through small gifts and patronage that gave the destitute some aid and the loyal young man a chance to rise politically. For revenue, the machine taxed the middle-class home owners and businessmen. Since these ward-based machines were also corrupt, they sold franchises and other special favours to certain businessmen who were willing in return to support city hall. Rebellion in the 1890s arose from coalitions of groups led by professionals such as clergymen and lawyers, supported by chambers of commerce and other associations of unfavoured local businessmen, which joined in demanding efficient and honest government in the interests of economic and social progress.

In the great wave of enthusiasm for the scientific society and the perfectibility of social institutions, around 1900, the reformers won victories in a number of cities and elected businesslike mayors, city managers or governing commissions. But in the long run the party machines had the votes. The middle class were more migratory than the poor, and their normal political interest in a city they might soon leave was slight. The chief businessmen came more and more to live outside the city limits, and only a few such as local bankers, large retailers, journalists and some professional men continued to battle for what they each wanted from municipal government.

The campaign for better housing in the first decade of the century was equally futile. A gifted young college graduate, Lawrence A. Veiller, played the deviant role of devoting his career to welfare and the improvement of slum conditions. Gradually winning the support of prominent New York businessmen, such as Robert W. DeForest of the Central Railroad of New Jersey, and the socially élite Charity Organisation Society, he secured a Tenement House Law in 1901 which became a model for the nation. Within a decade the ten largest cities were covered by such state laws, and a national association had been formed with a journal, *Housing*, edited by Veiller.

But, as in the case of much other progressive legislation, the courts came to the aid of property rights. A New York court handed down a leading decision that the owners of property, in this case Trinity Church, could only be required to make improvements within the economic possibilities of the existing structure. This meant that, while a new window here and there might be installed or water piped to another floor, the so-called old-law tenements continued to stand and operate. Furthermore, no new building conforming to the law could compete with these old rookeries in rent. Thus the net effect of the laws was to freeze the existing situation. Only the gradual expansion of population to new areas of the city offered some relief for the late-comers, who were then forced to pay rents above the minimums in the old areas.

Efforts to find a solution to the housing dilemma within the scope of the free market, however, continued. In the 1920s New York State, for example, offered tax exemption for new construction of minimum decent housing, but the few buildings constructed had rents too high to attract old-law tenement dwellers. By the 1930s there were more unsanitary and generally unsatisfactory slums than there had been in 1900, and relatively more than in any of the large cities of the western world. But the changing attitudes of the Great Depression finally started action. The Wagner–Steagel Act of 1937, providing federal subsidies for slum clearance, was the beginning of effective modification of the *laissez-faire* tradition in housing. In 1939, for the first time in American history, slums began to shrink and be replaced by low-rental, federally financed buildings.

While post-war Congresses continued limited federal subsidies for slum-clearance, problems appeared that had not been anticipated by earlier urban reformers. As old-stock Americans and successful newcomers moved to the suburbs there was no longer a shortage of housing in the central cities. The ghetto-dwellers who remained lived in deteriorating buildings, but, except for New York City, population density was not high. Meanwhile, the high-rise, exclusively residential apartment buildings, constructed with federal money and offering low rentals, proved an unsatisfactory alternative to the old run-down neighbourhoods. The skycrapers failed to house the same families they evicted or re-create the mixed communities of business and homes they had replaced, while their long empty corridors encouraged violent crime. With the recognized failure of this type of change, housing authorities in the 1960s gradually shifted, where it was possible, to the more successful plan of renovating existing dwellings.

Comprehensive city planning for future growth was a more complex challenge to the *laissez-faire* doctrine of control by the forces of the market. While central squares, parks, and street patterns had been planned in the nineteenth century, these had not usually interfered with the business life of cities, and where they had conflicted the parks and other tax-exempt uses of ground had given way. The idea of controlling future use of space by laws and ordinances grew with the progressive enthusiasm for a scientific society. But its impact was gradual. John Nolan of Cambridge, Massachusetts, and others started preaching its necessity around 1905, but only a handful of young or small cities such as San Diego, California, or Madison, Wisconsin, gave the planners a chance. Property values were too high in the older and larger centres to allow theorists to interfere with the course of adherence to the market.

The first important break in this sector of the front of *laissez-faire* came in New York City near the end of the old progressive movement. In 1916, over the protests of architects and real estate dealers, the State Legislature gave the city the right to zone for future development. Sections were divided into a number of industrial, commercial, or residential categories, and buildings over 150 feet high could use only a part of the air-space above their lots. In spite of themselves the architects, whose association had strongly protested at this infringement on their artistic freedom, had now to build gracefully set-back buildings rather than solid rows of slightly ornamented boxes. Other states followed New York until by 1931 37 per cent of the urban population lived in zoned communities. But zoning continued to have weaknesses. It could not undo the mistakes of the past, it prevented multi-purpose sub-communities, and strong political influence could, in most cities, win unwise exceptions of the law.

In the 1960s new small cities grew rapidly around the outlets and intersections of limited-access highways. Sometimes business offices and plants were restricted to an industrial park, shopping was in planned centres and housing in spreading developments. In other cases there was no planning beyond that of individual builders. These latter suggested that clean plants and attractive shops might create a new type of unzoned mixed neighbourhood.

Because of the expense involved, planning for better transportation within cities met even more resistance than zoning. At the turn of the century elevated and underground railways appeared to be the solution to moving people to work in the new skyscraper buildings that could mass a hundred thousand workers in a small area. But with inflation, from 1900 to 1920 a relatively static construction industry, and rapidly rising real wages in the building trades, underground railways, particularly, became prohibitively expensive. Only two or three cities in the United States attempted to extend underground transportation much beyond the plans adopted in the 1920s. Meanwhile, elevateds had proved so harmful to the value of adjacent property that the trend was to tear down rather than to extend them.

Successful inter-city or interstate cooperation led to a limited number of major tunnels and bridges over or under bays and rivers, but these facilities, which improved access to a city, made its internal traffic problems worse. From 1930 to about 1950 there was a virtual stalemate in remedies while conditions of movement within cities continued to deteriorate. Had the leaders of the New Deal been converted by Keynes they might have ended the depression by expenditures for underground railways, limited-access highways and housing, but this would have required a revolutionary change in cultural traditions and political doctrines, while the New Deal was mildly ameliorative, not revolutionary.

When, in the prosperous years after World War II, governments began again to spend money for urban improvement, limited-access highways inside the city rather than underground railways became the new formula for rapid transit. Although practically universally adopted, this solution inevitably deposited more and more automobiles in the central parts of the city, increasing both pollution of the air and uneconomic mid-city congestion. With a doubling of the number of motor vehicles between 1950 and 1970, survival of the cities obviously depended on important social change, but in the battles between urban taxpayers, commuters, users of office space, and home owners, all mediated by the city political machine, the results were still varying and uncertain in 1970. Cultural traditions of limited government and *laissez-faire* had persisted to a point where necessary change was going to be costly and difficult in both money and the disruption of homes in old-established neighbourhoods.

Replacement of slum areas by superhighways, educational institutions, or planned business areas, encouraged by a Federal Act of 1949, offering two-thirds of the cost involved in condemnation, led to new planning of previously untouched central cities, but it also affected slum-dwellers adversely. The neighbourhoods condemned may have been run down, but they were often communities that had been occupied for generations by particular ethnic groups. As a consequence there were frequently strong protests against such demolition, and city politicians were forced to decide between the business or professional interests wanting 'progress' but representing few votes, and substantial proportions of the electorate who wanted things as they were. Therefore, it was not uncommon for a mayor such as J. H. Tate of Philadelphia to oppose a central city highway link, financed by state and federal money, that would have large economic value, but destroy many neighbourhoods.

The ethnic ghettos, often islands of nationally and culturally homogeneous people within the urban complex, not necessarily composed of the poor, offered resistance to all types of urban change. If a new high school meant condemnation of homes, the displaced families would not be able to find other housing within the ghetto. They would become outcasts from their church, their neighbourhood, and one might say their nationality. The strife was greatest where blacks, through federal housing, encroached on the schools and streets of old, well-established ethnic groups. Such problems explain strong support in some northern urban areas for the reactionary, racist George Wallace in 1968.

As suggested by these examples, the effect of city life on social roles was not as uniform and simple as thought by early urban sociologists. In general, the sanctioning groups for urban roles were more impersonal and changeable, which made for easier deviation or innovation, but at the cost of the reinforcement that could come from the positive face-to-face sanctions for good performance. At one extreme the city-dweller might suffer from anomie, or feeling of the lack of any role-set really interested in his performance. With the development of substantial mobile homes many families were completely free to change geographical environment and role-sets while taking the familiar household aspects of their family life with them. At the other extreme a city-dweller could operate in a closed, segregated world such as a university or an old neighbourhood community that offered some of the positive and negative sanctioning force of a country village. The large, well-educated middle group, tolerably adjusted to frequent moves in either cities or suburbs, represented an historically new element in the population whose role-playing propensities were still not clear in 1970.

One effect of any large aggregations of population in a developing society is important for change. More people with specialized knowledge or skills are brought together, and they reinforce each other in innovations and improvements. In a time of rapid technological advance business firms needing such help clustered in the major metropolitan areas where they could 'externalize' such costs and risks by contracting with outside specialists. The demographic trends of the last half of the twentieth century indicated increasing concentration of all social activity in metropolitan areas.

CHAPTER IX

FROM FAMILY TO INSTITUTIONAL
SECURITY

The feeling of security is unquestionably related to early character-formation which requires study by psychologists and psychoanalysts rather than historians. Yet later preception of social probabilities and possibilities can modify such characteristics to a degree that justifies historians in speaking of secure classes or optimistic periods in the life of a nation. Study of a small city about 1950, for example, demonstrated through questionnaires given to a very large random sample of lower to lower middle-class people that they felt themselves more secure than their parents had been.[1] Obviously, in the preceding generation there had been an interaction between external social change and internalized attitudes.

In 1900, American industrial workers, surrounded by an increasingly affluent society, were by external standards miserably insecure. The contradiction had been fostered by a dogmatic belief that, since each man should take care of himself, poverty was a sign of immorality, which was coupled with wages too low to allow any adequate saving. In practice the first source of reliance for care of the old or disabled was their children or close relatives; another possibility was that a benevolent employer might provide a low-paid sedentary job, and the final resort was to the state poorhouse. For most of those who lost the ability to work each of the resources was unsatisfactory. For two-thirds

[1] Thomas C. Cochran 'Foreword', Sidney Goldstein, *The Norristown Study*, Philadelphia: University of Pennsylvania Press, 1961, pp. viii–ix.

of the population, the security offered by the family farm had gone and nothing had filled its place.

Adequate voluntary saving proved practically impossible for even a moderately well-paid worker. The claims of home and family (the primary role-set) for immediate needs were always likely to be more pressing than the resolution to put a certain sum in the bank. Even in the rare instances of the dedicated saver, the interest on the small accumulation possible from the total lifetime earnings of no more than $20,000 of a semi-skilled worker around 1900 would not go far in providing support for an indefinite period of enforced idleness. Each of the other solutions, also, had severe weaknesses: children resented having to support parents when they were already experiencing a peak of expenditure for raising their own sons and daughters; while some small employers were benevolent, others were not, and big impersonal companies had no pension systems; home relief had generally been ended in the 1870s, and poorhouses were deliberately made unattractive.

As the upper classes became aroused about the evils and dangers of industrial society, able women such as Jane Addams, Florence Kelley and Lillian D. Wald devoted themselves to giving aid and seeking legislative action. The first successful campaigns for security by state law won compensation for workers in case of industrial accidents. Industry and railroads had developed with the philosophy that men should take care of themselves, yet with 25,000 deaths and a million injuries a year, industrial accidents had become a major social problem. The common-law doctrines of contributory negligence and the possible responsibility of fellow workers blocked effective recovery of damages, but in any case legal action was too expensive for people without income. Starting with a New York Act of 1910, the states passed laws compelling employers to carry insurance that would provide automatic payments in case of accidents. The initial reaction of the courts was to regard such acts as a deprivation of property without due process of law, prohibited by the 14th Amendment to the federal constitution, but by 1913 the drafters of laws and the judges had reached compromises that permitted legally valid workman's compensation acts.

As late as 1928 only half a dozen states had laws providing small pensions for the aged, and only those of Montana and Wisconsin were actually operating. While a number of states adopted such legislation in 1929 and 1930, bringing the total to 29, many of the laws depended on county co-operation, so that of 6,500,000 people over 65 years of age only 180,000 received state support. Consequently, the United States entered the great depression with a highly inadequate and uneven level of governmental social security, one that compared poorly with the provisions of other industrial nations.[1]

Private pension plans might, and, according to the free enterprise tradition, should have come to the rescue. But, here again, the prosperity of the upper-income groups in the 1920s reinforced the doctrine of self-help in delaying action. With the higher real wages prevailing after the price collapse of 1920, and the rising stock market, the properly diligent were expected, more than ever before, to become financially secure through saving. Only railroads, a few banks, and less than 150 industrial companies out of some 200,000 adopted pension plans. They were almost all non-contributory and hence subject to change by the company, and required long periods of service. In all about 150,000 people received pensions in 1930 from some private source.[2] In the depression, while some new private plans were instituted, many old ones disappeared.

Before 1929 only a few business leaders realized that, by not assuming more of the burden for the welfare and security of its employees, free enterprise was seriously failing to protect its philosophy of voluntarism from an irresistible demand for state action. Efforts at cooperative voluntary planning were, in case after case, blocked by the same philosophy of freedom of action that gave them birth. Too many proprietors refused to assume

[1] John R. Commons and Associates, *History of Labor in the United States, 1896–1932*, New York: Macmillan, 1935, Vol. III, pp. 385, 613–15.
[2] Commons, *op. cit.*, Vol. III, p. 385.

burdens that would diminish profits when they could not be assured that all their competitors would do likewise, or, as the great speaker at dinners for businessmen, Chauncey Depew, put it: 'The trouble with gentlemen's agreements is that only a few of those present are gentlemen.'

Perhaps it was well that the United States did not adopt the Latin-American or Japanese forms of security through business paternalism. While, in the view of management, such schemes were cloaked in the approved mantle of voluntarism, they were usually, in fact, coupled with an authoritarianism increasingly repugnant to democratically inclined employees. At all events, as the United States headed into its greatest depression, the voluntarist doctrine, accompanied by little welfare activity, still dominated the business and political élites including the doctrine's staunch, idealistic exponent, President Hoover.

What happened next in the history of social security can only be understood in the context of the destructive force of the Great Depression on the traditional value placed on self-help, and on the doctrine that poverty indicated vice. Undoubtedly the United States would ultimately have adjusted to the obvious human needs of urban industralism, as had other nations of the western world, but the change would have been much slower. The degree of resistance to federal unemployment relief even at the bottom of the depression illustrated the strength of the old attitudes.

Because of great over-optimism in boom periods and a weak banking system, the United States had always had severe fluctuations in the business cycle. In both the 1870s and the 1890s depressions had been so severe that they produced mild response from the federal government, but the help was directed to supporting financial markets, not the unemployed, who depended on relatives and charity. In both of these depressions the agricultural sector of the economy had been far larger in relation to the industrial, and the western world situation had been less disastrous, so that recovery had ultimately come by the classic economic means of renewed investment in producer goods which increased employment and brought prosperity. In the twentieth century the foreign orders of World War I had ended a depression that had started in 1913, and in the collapse of 1920, the backlog of unsatisfied demand at lower prices was sufficient to make the depression brief. Fortified by the Maginot Line of the new Federal Reserve System, all but a handful of business leaders in 1929 thought depressions the results of errors that would not recur, and dire poverty as a thing of the past.

In fact, the United States was in a more vulnerable position economically than its business analysts, save one or two like Roger Babson, were willing to recognize. Increasing exports that helped to sustain the quite moderate prosperity of the late 1920s were possible only on the basis of a large volume of foreign lending and investment or, in other words, on the continuance of an easy money market in the United States. Meanwhile, not only was there no reduction in tariffs that would permit a larger volume of imports, but in 1930 there was a substantial increase in tariff rates. Hence exports would only hold up as long as foreign securities were easy to sell. In 1927, '28 and '29 the domestic economy was operating well below its maximum capacity, there was considerable unemployment, and by mid-1929 construction and some other sensitive indexes were headed down.

The boom was living on an unprecedented flow of 'call money' into Wall Street from both domestic and foreign sources, and an unreasoning over-optimism regarding the future profits of large corporations or, as a leading banker later testified, 'lots of atmosphere'. In role language, the market operators were to a large extent each other's role-sets and they engaged in mutual reinforcement which had little connection with the real world. In spite of the ominous portents in external reality, the speculators reached their greatest heights of optimism, nearly doubling the average price of 'blue-chip' securities between June and September 1929. Unfortunately for the future of the nation, all the bad financial practices of the ages reappeared in Wall Street. One that was to prove the most serious was that even conservative bankers, pillars of the financial system, shared the false belief in the stability of stock market values, and made individual loans of millions of dollars secured by thousands of shares of vulnerable issues of common stock, which were to prove unsaleable in a panicky or even 'thin' market.

The dependence of exports on new financing, and the weakness of the big bank loans secured by stock market securities in particularly, made the panics of October and November more far-reaching in their subsequent effects than superficial analysts forecast. The latter, who had no conception of the quantity of under-secured bank loans, contended that, while by December stock prices had been cut in half, the average was still as high as in 1928, and they saw no reason why prosperity should not continue. In public President Hoover was one of the optimists, but in private, sensing to some degree the international, if not the domestic, banking situation, he pleaded with business leaders to go on with expansion and maintain wages in order to avoid disaster, and voluntarism worked as usual; each man hoped that the others would follow the good advice, while he cut costs and commitments.

Now the threat of insecurity came gradually to apply to a majority of the families of the nation, middle-class as well as blue-collar, substantial investors as well as those without savings, and ultimately to the central corporate structure of capitalism. Both declining business and unemployment had two phases that nearly coincided. In the first period, from 1929 to the autumn of 1930, the depression did not seem much different from its historic predecessors. But from October of that year the banking system began to collapse from the pressures of rigid banking laws that compelled the posting of bank capital to secure delinquent loans or non-paying mortgages. Bank failures in the interior, each tying-up the money of depositors, culminated in December in the failure of a large New York City bank, unfortunately named the Bank of the United States. By early 1931, the American contraction of bank credit was being severely felt in Germany, which had become particularly dependent on short-term loans and investments from the United States. Alive to the dangers of the situation, France called in her short-term German credits in March and the world-wide financial crisis began.

From here on, Hoover was partly justified in saying that the depression was a world-wide result of the unsettled financial obligations of World War I, but apart from a delayed declaration of a moratorium on the payment of international war debts to the United States, he took no active part in alleviating the situation.[1] He also continued his belief in voluntarism at home. Told as early as June of 1931 that the banks of the United States needed massive government help, he suggested instead a voluntary credit association through which strong banks would help the weak. This, of course, did not happen, and, threatened by a collapse of the whole system, Hoover finally agreed late in 1931 to sponsor the bill for the Reconstruction Finance Corporation.

This federal lending agency with a two billion dollar appropriation from Congress is one of the great symbolic milestones in United States history. It marks the surrender of the concept of 'the self-regulating economy' by an administration representing its strongest adherents, one that had resisted the introduction of institutionalized security for workers, investors, or small bankers and other businessmen, and had only abandoned voluntarism and invoked the institutional power of government to save the main corporate structure. From the standpoint of the doctrine of self-help, rescuing big corporations was less demoralizing than saving individuals, but even in this action Hoover was still the 'man convinced against his will'. By vetoing half a dozen measures for economic relief or institutionalized security in the spring of 1932, he still refused to take the steps necessary to prevent a complete breakdown of the banking system the following year.

While this brief sketch of the depression has indicated the problems of the families whose security had rested on stocks, bonds, or bank deposits, the aim has also been to provide a

---

[1] He serves as an excellent example of how conditioning limits the actor's perception and range of subjective construction. Hoover had at his disposal literally undreamed-of financial power, but he could not imagine its use. His internalized sanctions and his role-sets strictly limited his potential for innovation.

background for the shift toward institutional security for unemployed, destitute individuals.

Early in the depression the President had announced his voluntaristic formula for aid. The first recourse should be to the family, next to the neighbours, third to the landlord, then to private charity and only ultimately to local government. Needless to say, in a great depression affecting agriculture even more than industry, these recourses, except for landlords and local government, were nearly useless. Landlords would allow rent to accumulate because eviction cost money and no other tenants were in sight. Local governments had to try to do something because, as private charity was quickly exhausted, the burden came to rest on them. But local resources were often utterly inadequate to carry the burden of unemployment which in some heavy-industry towns amounted to over 80 per cent of the former working population.

As general unemployment rose to more than a quarter of the labour force and hours worked fell to two-fifths of those in 1929, states as well as incorporated local governments reached bankruptcy. Property-owners let their tax liabilities accumulate, municipal credit approached points of no return, and many states reached their constitutional limits of borrowing. Furthermore, the burden of relief was very unevenly distributed. States such as those of the Middle Atlantic and Middle Western areas which produced most of the durable goods had far worse unemployment than the farm states. Ironically, this did not always redound to the benefit of the destitute in the rural areas because, while states like New York made heroic efforts to maintain welfare, some of the southern states did very little. One could succumb to the diseases of undernourishment as readily as in an unplanted cotton field as in an urban slum.

Meanwhile, in 1931, the President had assured the nation that 'if the time should ever come that the voluntary agencies are unable to find resources to prevent hunger and suffering I will ask the aid of every resource of the Federal Government'. Even as he spoke the time had already come, and by 1932 it was long past, yet the President, refusing to admit that the situation existed, recalls Herbert A. Simon's remark that it can be contended that the actor's 'perceived world is fantastically different from the "real world" '.[1]

It is not difficult to find reasons for Hoover's quite literally 'fantastic' failure in perception. An obvious factor is that he was surrounded by wealthy, conservative men in his Cabinet and among his other advisers who did not want to face the appalling reality, and few men are likely to overcome the pressure of their intimate role-sets when the latter reinforce the internalized sanction or emotional bias of the actor. On this basis, Hoover can be excused as a normally benevolent man who was the victim of strongly held beliefs reinforced by his personal environment.

But for politicians in the top ranks of both political parties there were substantial economic reasons for overlooking the inadequacies of relief. State and local taxation was largely confined to real property and, therefore, had both relatively low maximum limits and did not hit the major resources of the prosperous which were in stocks, bonds, salaries and other contracts. The Federal Government, however, would raise additional revenue largely from corporation and graduated income taxes that would bear most heavily on high incomes and the world of business. An additional factor was that the bonds of state agencies and municipalities were tax-exempt and, therefore, a welcome recourse for those with high incomes, whereas federal bonds were not. Hence the rich—and in a broad use of the term this included almost all successful national politicians—recoiled from the type of taxes that would result from a federal assumption of the burdens of relief.

In the presidential campaign of 1932 Franklin D. Roosevelt was forced by the condition of some 12 to 15 million unemployed (they were not officially counted at that time) to advocate federal assumption of the major burden of relief, whereas Hoover campaigned on the basis of limited grants to the states; but in economic conceptions, in general, there was little difference

[1] See the discussion in Chapter I.

between either the candidates or the other leaders of the two parties. The real hope of the voters for recovery under Roosevelt rested on his confident and pragmatic attitudes, as against Hoover's aura of unsympathetic, austere idealism. Since, as John N. Garner put it, Roosevelt had only to stay alive in order to be elected, he had no need to commit himself to specific policies. Except for a single speech in September, largely written by the economist Rexford G. Tugwell, in which Roosevelt forecast expanded federal activity, he and Hoover argued about prohibition or minor issues.

While Roosevelt came to Washington in March, 1933, pledged to almost nothing beyond repeal of prohibition, adequate relief and aid to the farmer, the state of the nation forced prompt legislative actions which all resulted in increased institutional security. Unable to sustain drains on their capital for bad debts, and on their cash reserves from withdrawals by cautious depositors, the banks were closed by a presidential order of March 5th, accepted by Congress on the basis of his powers in a national emergency. While, under a new banking act, they were gradually reopened without much change in the general system, each bank could join in a plan for insurance of depositors' accounts up to $5,000. The investor was given more security by divorcing investment from commercial banking, and by forcing disclosure of all-important information regarding new security issues. Federal farm and home loan agencies guaranteed the banks in re-financing mortgages and giving householders the security of long-term amortization by low monthly payments. A complicated agricultural programme was designed to give the farm-owner a more secure income, although tenants were left to fend for themselves. Cut-throat competition which was ruining small business, and wage cutting which was impoverishing labour and reducing consumer spending were met by the National Industrial Recovery Act, offering a degree of security to all business firms which would subscribe to codes for fair practice.

Meanwhile, relief had been underwritten by federal funds, and an emergency relief administration established in Washington under Harry Hopkins. Even on this basis relief was still niggardly and far from enough to re-stimulate the economy through consumer spending. But among all of the so-called brain trust that advised Roosevelt, only Hugh Johnson, Rexford Tugwell and Frances Perkins had Keynesian ideas regarding government spending. The others shared Roosevelt's belief that economy and a balanced budget were political shibboleths that must be respected.

In the early phase of passage of legislation for institutional security, often referred to as the 100 days or the honeymoon period, support for the administration had been bi-partisan. But, as congressional liberals passed legislation for devaluation of the dollar and strict regulation of security markets, the Republicans and business in general broke with the President. In the congressional election of 1934, most of the newspapers, businessmen, and other members of the upper income groups backed the Republicans and, contrary to the general trend of non-presidential elections, they were overwhelmingly defeated. The administration now had a liberal majority in Congress large enough to pass any reasonable reform legislation.

As Democratic analysts surveyed the victory they readily concluded that security had been the major issue. The people felt safer with Roosevelt's friends than with his opponents. Harry Hopkins, a life-long social worker, and other advisers now argued cogently that, since security was political magic, the people should have more of it. A short-run result was the Works Progress Administration, designed to re-employ skilled workers of all types, to prevent their losing their abilities, and administered by the man who was to become the President's closest adviser, Harry Hopkins. The long-run result was the Social Security Act of 1935.

If the Reconstruction Finance Corporation marked the symbolic beginning of the 'Welfare State', the Social Security Act made it a reality. The President rated it as his most important achievement. It marked the final political defeat of the historic American belief that it was socially demoralizing for the Federal

Government permanently to support the old or unfortunate. The law itself was designed for the future, not as a panacea for the depression. Old-age pensions were to be based on an insurance plan under which employers and employees would contribute equally in amounts that would increase over the years and gradually make the system self-supporting. Until 1941 the fund would be used only to supplement state pension plans. To those who contributed, unemployment compensation would be paid for a limited period, at the end of which time the worker without a job would go on federal relief.

Because in the beginning the collections would exceed the benefits, the immediate impact of the law was mildly deflationary, and until the late 1940s it covered only a part of the working force. Its economic impact was also held back by the actuarial method of accounting which related benefits to premium payments. Since neither employers nor younger workers wanted sharp increases in the social security taxes, the benefits received by the average aged couple were below what the Bureau of Labor Statistics set as the poverty line. There were signs by the 1960s, however, that the old belief that no one should get what they had not earned was weakening and that, once military expenditures were less demanding, there might be large increases in social security minimums that would bring them up to a fair subsistence level irrespective of the amounts paid in. Meanwhile, in 1965, any actuarial balance in social security accounts was, no doubt, permanently lost by adding limited amounts of free medical care for those over sixty-five.

Passage of these social security laws was, in itself, a major social change, brought about by the pressures of new types of occupations and ways of living which, over the span of half a century, had made the older institutions increasingly dysfunctional. Their psychological effects, particularly those of more adequate old-age pensions, unemployment insurance and medicare, should be studied more in nations in which they have had a longer history than in the United States. Surely continual high geographical mobility that broke down family security in America was a cause, and still freer movement away from home and relatives probably an effect of the new situation. In this respect social security joined with the other forces of metropolitan society, such as nurseries for infant care and longer schooling, in undermining the strength of family ties, while the automobile, television, and more family vacation trips were working somewhat in the opposite direction.

Instead of replacing the movement for private pension plans, social security, aided by the post-war demands of organized labour, gave the idea of institutional planning for old age a fresh impetus. More upper-middle-class spending in relation to saving than in earlier periods was also, in part, a reflection of more, in some cases highly, adequate institutionalized security for old age. Until late in their careers, many corporate managers made no personal provision for the future through private investment, except for repayments of packaged mortgages on homes which appeared in the capital markets not as personal saving but as money in the hands of banks or other institutional investors.

The conservatives of the 1930s, who opposed the welfare state on the basis of demoralization of workers and high costs, feeling sure that they were resisting portentous change, never foresaw all of the effects of the changed relationships in spending, saving, and taxes. In addition to largely shifting control of new capital from individuals to institutions, the altered tax structure helped radically to change the performance of the economy. Up to 1935 the tax system of the Federal Government, based on tariffs and excises, bore heavily on consumers and more lightly on those prosperous enough to do substantial private saving. As a result, from the 1890s on, the incidence of federal taxation was one of the major forces behind a tendency for saving to outrun investment in domestic enterprises employing labour, or, put another way, making it difficult to maintain a consumer demand that would justify the expansion of productive equipment made possible by the available capital. This was particularly obvious in the late 1920s, when unemployment rose and consumer prices actually declined in a boom period. Stagnation was the great menace.

From the tax law that accompanied the social security bill of 1935, nicknamed the 'soak the rich' act, the incidence of federal taxation shifted sharply up the income scale. World War II accentuated the process and accustomed business corporations to paying over half their net income in taxes, and individuals to parting with as much as nine-tenths. While in the 1960s maximum individual taxes were reduced to the 70 per cent level, and a number of the very rich, by keeping their money in real estate and tax-exempt bonds, avoided income taxes altogether, the net effect of the change was greatly to curtail private saving in the upper income brackets. Meanwhile, during the period from 1940 on, higher real wages led to large increases in consumer demand by those in the middle to lower income groups. The two forces together helped to produce a capitalism in which too low a rate of expansion of the facilities of production and inflation, rather than stagnation from over-saving, became the bogey-man, not only of the United States, but of western world capitalism as a whole.

Increase in bargaining power which continually raised wages, still to be discussed, was an important ingredient in the new 'institutional capitalism' which constituted one of the major social changes in world history. We must explore further the causal elements in the growth of high consumption which to some observers made possessions, not religion, 'the Opium of the People'.

CHAPTER X

DISRUPTIVE CHANGE

Sudden or disruptive social change logically follows from abrupt widespread shifts in role-playing that shatter outmoded but important institutions. Historically such change appears to need impetus from unusual external forces. The single individual may be highly motivated to change roles and institutions, as the banker Marriner Eccles was when he came to Washington in 1933, but the continuous resistance of role-sets gradually eroded his plans and made his ultimate personal contribution to change seem small in comparison to his initial aims.[1] *Sub-rosa* communication may produce in many men a desire to alter the institutions that govern some of their roles, but usually it requires a strike situation, a *coup d'état*, a national calamity, a war, or a depression to bring together and motivate a group that will reinforce each other in daring to attack powerful role-sets guarding the established order.

The tendency toward inertia in tolerable situations is illustrated in the perpetuation of a number of the attitudes of American businessmen and their political representatives, attitudes already anachronistic in the late nineteenth century, until the panic of 1929. Although World War I had brought some new ideas to business and politics, including temporary reliance by some on government agencies and trade associations, the expanded government operations, such as railroad administration or control over fuel and some prices, were speedily liquidated, and the trade associations found their new cooperative activities checked by

[1] Marriner S. Eclces, *Beckoning Frontiers: Public and Personal Recollections*, New York: Knopf, 1951, pp. 128 ff.

both unresponsive members and the anti-trust laws. The major change in the world financial situation of the United States from being a large net debtor to an unprecedentedly big net creditor unfortunately had little basic effect on either business or political institutions. The consequences of the war on the nation came less from the economic results of high corporate profits from 1915 on, or from a year and a half of feverish and confused preparation for military production, than from the psychological reflection of post-war European disillusionment on artists, reformers, and intellectuals, and from the fear of communism in wide sections of the middle-class public. But in the economically buoyant twenties the Red scare died down and the artists, intellectuals, or reformers had little effect on the main stream of American life.

The political and economic atmosphere of the twenties was one of nostalgia for a vaguely defined past and firm belief in the future marvels to be expected from old-fashioned, unrestricted free enterprise. Business, in effect, proclaimed itself responsible for the progress of the nation, and in small cities throughout the interior critics of this beneficent system were treated as un-American pariahs. While vestiges of the progressive attitude remained in some of the states, the national government de-emphasized regulation, and Herbert Hoover, Secretary of Commerce, and reputedly under-secretary of everything else, preached his doctrine of voluntary business co-operation for the common good.

Thus the panic of 1929 and the ensuing depression disrupted the mood and accepted sanctions of the nation with more violence than would have been possible in any earlier period. By February 1932, when that erstwhile popular sage, Henry Ford, remarked, 'We have come to the end of an era of waste and inefficiency', the American dream of an economic system superior to that of any other nation, of a mission to set an example for the world, which had gradually taken shape in the mid-nineteenth century had, it then seemed, come to an end.[1]

[1] Allan Nevins and Frank Ernest Hill, *Ford: Decline and Rebirth 1933–1962*, New York: Scribner, 1962, p. 1.

Over five thousand bank-failures from 1930 through 1932, and Congressional hearings in 1932 and 1933 exposing business dishonesty and malpractice in high places, gave the formerly complacent middle class a further traumatic shock. Since in their communities the presidents and directors of the insolvent banks had been the leading citizens, their repudiation pulled up the roots of the local systems of power and prestige. Old sanctions and role-sets were gone, and it was not clear what or who would take their place. Reacting from the near-worship of business in the previous decade, much of the public now suspected every pronouncement or effort coming from business leaders, and since such proposals were, in general, wrong or futile, the public was justified.

The major plan of the new Roosevelt administration for the resuscitation of business, the National Industrial Recovery Act, of the spring of 1933, was a mixed set of aids put together in great haste. The President himself had no plan for business recovery beyond the effects of added financial security and the 'reflation' of prices through agricultural and monetary policies. Businessmen, in general, wanted suspension or repeal of the anti-trust laws so that they could check ruinous competition by forming cartels to control prices. The immediate spur to action, however, came from the representatives of organized labour in Congress who introduced a bill for the thirty-hour week. The prospect that the bill would pass aroused the administration and business organizations such as the national Chamber of Commerce to prepare a counter-proposal.

The bill that resulted from compromises between the friends of business and labour tried to give each side some of what it wanted. The anti-trust laws were suspended so that firms in each industry could draw up a code that would fix prices and regulate conditions of production. Employers signing a code must agree to the eight-hour day and bargain collectively with representatives of labour. The bill passed in June, and ultimately nearly all industries either voluntarily adopted a special code or were coerced by strong administrative pressure into accepting a standard form of agreement concerning labour.

From first to last the basic problem was labour relations. The idea of granting bargaining power to labour equal to that of management struck at the authoritarian, hierarchical principle basic to the institutions of business. Always opposing independent unionism, employers had restricted it largely to the skilled crafts, which involved only a small fraction of all workers. In the prosperous 1920s this minority group declined slowly in size, and in the depression fell away rapidly. By 1933 a smaller percentage of the labour force belonged to national unions than at any time since the early years of the century. Management could now hope that the Great Depression would break down the whole national union structure, as had the prolonged unemployment of the 1870s. Consequently, the labour provisions of the NLRA were agreed to with great reluctance, or not at all in the case of the automobile industry, and even if agreed to *pro forma*, management hoped the labour clause, Section 7A, would prove unenforcible and unconstitutional.

On the other side, within the American Federation of Labor, a few leaders of essentially industry-wide unions such as John L. Lewis of the United Mine Workers, and David Dubinsky and Sidney Hillman of the ladies' and men's clothing workers, saw the law as a chance to spread industrial unionism to the previously unorganized major industries. During this period leadership of the movement was taken over by Lewis, a towering, beetle-browed, evangelical speaker of great force, who was nevertheless a pragmatist with generally conservative leanings.[1] The result of the new campaign was four years of warfare between labour and management, the results of which far overshadow in significance the brief period of business regulation under the NRA codes.

The progress of organization was hindered by opposition from the skilled crafts in the A.F. of L., continued depression, and unemployment, as well as by the strong counter-measures of

[1] The situation illustrates the direction given by cultural conditioning to the terms of social conflict. The businessmen were contending for authority that their upbringing had convinced them was vital. The unionists were led by a man quite similar to the businessmen he opposed: a man of powerful action but weaker ideas, ready to accept what would work, intent on maintaining his own income, and wholly opposed to revolution.

employers. From July of 1933 to the Supreme Court ruling that NRA was unconstitutional in May 1935, industrial unionists gained only slightly and in small business rather than in large. Many big corporations started company unions and met the formal requirements of Section 7A by bargaining with these internally controlled organizations. Such unions had grown rapidly in World War I, when bargaining was forced by the government on war contractors, and between 1933 and 1935 they doubled in membership to 2,500,000. Thousands of espionage agents were also distributed among the workers to discover secret organizers for the outside unions, who were promptly fired.

In the summer of 1935 Senator Robert F. Wagner of New York, in many ways the principal legislative figure of the Great Depression, was able, with the mild approval of the President, to put through Congress a strong National Labor Relations Act. On the basis that the products made by their workers appeared in interstate commerce, the law placed stringent limitations on such employers. Its provisions included prohibition of any activity by an employer designed to affect the choice of bargaining agents by his workers, and compelled him to bargain for all the workers with the union that won a majority at an election held at a time of its own choosing. Since the Supreme Court in 1935 and 1936 continued severely to restrict the commerce powers of Congress, practically everyone, including labour leaders, thought the law would be declared unconstitutional. Consequently, business in general paid little attention to the NLRA, called the Wagner Act, and labour leaders had small hope of effective support from the National Labor Relations Board it had created.

The event that touched off the great upsurge of unionism in major industries was the sweeping re-election of Roosevelt in 1936, along with liberal Democratic governors and members of Congress. Business leaders through the Liberty League and the National Association of Manufacturers had deliberately made the election a test of their principles of free enterprise and self-help against the President's belief in controls and aids for the 'under-privileged'. Relying much on a poll that showed a majority of telephone subscribers for Republican Alfred D. Landon, the upper classes had actually deluded themselves into thinking that they would win, and their ultimate inability to secure even 40 per cent of the popular vote, and only two small states in the electoral college, left them as emotionally disorganized as had the initial depression. The basic institutions of the United States as the business élite had seen them for hundreds of years were no longer viable at the polls.

Or so it seemed, but like most initial attacks upon basic cultural values this questioning of the sanctions that had been major guides for American action was soon overcome. Apparently destroyed by the force of events from 1933 to 1936, the old sanctions had partly recovered their strength by 1938, and the New Deal was at an end. Meanwhile, however, a lasting social change had been made in labour relations.

Proceeding on the basis of a return toward prosperity and political support rather than on that of the dubious Wagner Act, the leaders of the A.F. of L. Committee for Industrial Organization won spectacular strikes for union recognition in most of the automotive industry. Analysis, by the historian Sidney Fine, of the key victory—the sit-down strike against General Motors at Flint, Michigan—makes it appear unlikely that labour could have succeeded with less friendly political leaders than the state's Governor, Frank Murphy, and President Roosevelt. Three times Murphy failed to use the military power of the state to enforce court injunctions, while the President urged the leaders of General Motors to bargain with John L. Lewis.

The success of the CIO unions, now expelled by the A.F. of L., in gaining the right to represent all workers in a number of major industries appeared to be a triumph for communist or radical leadership. That the same unions, reunited and secure in their bargaining positions, in the more affluent society of thirty years later would be essentially conservative supporters of the established order seemed highly unlikely.

In the late winter and spring of 1937, while labour was winning in motors, rubber, and steel through its own physical and political strength, the President's bill for large additions to the personnel of the Supreme Court was before Congress. This fact, plus the President's large popular vote of 1936, the legal weakness of some of the court decisions restricting the commerce power, and the close balance between liberal and conservative factions on the Court, all contributed in April, 1937, to a surprising affirmation of the constitutionality of the National Labor Relations Act. Remaining as the law of the land for another decade, this Act, and government support of union organization in World War II in return for a no-strike pledge, laid the basis for the modern labour movement in the United States.

The withdrawal of the Court bill in the face of its certain defeat, and the onset of an unprecedentedly rapid slump in business in mid-1937, directly connected with the President's efforts to conciliate the conservatives by reducing spending, greatly injured the prestige of the administration. While in 1938 the liberals in Congress, by trading votes with southern conservatives, were still able to put through a fair employment act involving the first national minimum wage, balanced by a new farm bill, the administration had lost its power for further reform. On the basis of the deep depression of 1937 and 1938 the New Deal was an economic failure, and many citizens were more discouraged than in 1933.

The immediate trouble is easy to explain in the light of later neo-Keynesian economics. The President had never been convinced that prosperity could be brought back by spending, and he regarded deficits as a political liability. Neither by personal conversation nor by urgent letters was Keynes ever able to penetrate the President's non-theoretical mind. In this respect Roosevelt was not more obtuse than a majority of academic economists in the United States, who for as much as a decade resisted the clear understanding of the relations of income, demand, saving and investment that Keynes had presented.

The major Keynesian revelation was that business decisions to invest depended on demand, not on the amount of saving. Hence, governmental economizing in a depression was the road to further decline, and spending, from whatever source, was necessary to create the demand that would encourage business-men to make new investments. Among types of government spending, public works were the most desirable because they involved long-run contracts creating a demand that the suppliers could count on for a number of years. But expenditures for public works by Hoover and Roosevelt had been increased only moderately, since both Presidents had seen such projects as merely a way of spreading work, not of creating prosperity. Looking at all levels of government together, such spending declined from 1930 to 1936 and rose in the latter year chiefly through the resumption of necessary state and local outlays: WPA, the largest spending programme of the New Deal, was strictly limited by both short-term appropriations and restrictions on the use of capital, and hence gave no incentive for new industrial investment.

The depression from 1937 to 1939 was undoubtedly precipi-tated by strenuous efforts at balancing the budget through cutting off billions of dollars in federal spending, partly from wrong economic views, but also to gain conservative support for the Court bill. The Roosevelt reasoning was always political rather than economic. Keynes wrote to him early in 1938, in what must be one of the most critical letters ever sent by a world-famous figure to a friendly chief-of-state, that the President's economies were endangering capitalism all over the world.

Yet, in spite of the short-run economic impotence of the New Deal, the Great Depression, as a whole, had such enduring socio-economic effects that it marked the beginning of a new period in United States history. Starting with the Reconstruction Finance Corporation of 1932, the federal government assumed increasing responsibility for the general welfare, as illustrated in the new security given to home-owners, investors, workers, the aged and the unemployed. Taxation and expenditure were redesigned in a way that made consumption larger in relation to saving. A strong labour movement was created in manufacturing, mining and transportation, and farmers with staple crops were given annual subsidies on the basis of acreage restriction that were still the rule in 1970. The Tennessee Valley Authority, by demonstrating what inexpensive hydro-electric power could do to improve agriculture, became the precedent for additional dams and rural electrification.

With little possibility of business employment because of the depression, young lawyers and potential executives sought positions in the rapidly expanding bureaucracy in Washington. Since, in the long run, government positions on all levels continued to increase and were later joined by permanently expanded military services, the United States developed, for the first time, the kind of attractive permanent careers in public service common to most other nations. The rise of scientific research in the postwar years, largely financed by the federal government, opened still another non-business avenue to high social prestige. By the mid-1960s only about one-fifth of college graduates were directly entering business. This shift away from the extreme importance of business as the road to success, initiated by the Great Depression, brought the United States of 1970 closer than ever before to the pluralistic systems of values and prestige of the other western nations.

While World War I had involved a relatively brief effort that had little lasting effect on economics or politics in the United States, World War II was a wholly engrossing commitment which both released energies held back by depression and firmly established the adjustments to industrialism made by the New Deal. Farm productivity was unleashed, new industry, with capital largely supplied by government, spread to the urban fringes, the additional workers recruited for war production became union members, government planning and regulation came to be taken for granted, and taxes which all but consumed large corporate or private incomes were accepted as necessary evils. The excessive pressure for consumer goods, arising largely from full employment and pay for overtime, demonstrated how high consumption could be if everyone was well paid—the Keynesian truth that Roosevelt had either never grasped, or else never dared to act on politically. The war taught both politicians and economists fundamental lessons about the operation of the advanced industrial state that they would never have absorbed from any amount of Keynesian argument.

After experiencing wartime administration and costs, people readily accepted post-war levels of public employment and federal expenditures that would have seemed outrageous to the opponents of the New Deal. In 1946 a conservative Congress passed a law declaring the federal government's responsibility for trying to maintain full employment, and gave the President a council of economic advisers with the rather ironic mandate of regularly suggesting how to control the economy in the interest of free enterprise. The welfare state with its system of values was now an accepted institution of the United States.[1]

Other continuing governmental situations arose from the long-run effects of the Great Depression and World War II. The fear of the large planters in the South, who were often active in politics, that agricultural subsidies would be cut back, and the fear of many businessmen that the nearly continuously Democratic Congress would enact legislation favourable to labour, drew the representatives of these groups together in a planter-business alliance that could usually command a congressional majority. The strength of the alliance was demonstrated many times. In 1947, the Taft–Hartley Act, ending the closed shop by majority vote and placing restrictions on picketing, was re-passed over President Truman's veto, in spite of only a slim Republican majority in Congress. Again, in 1959, after twelve years of attempts to amend Taft–Hartley in ways favourable to labour, a Congress with a large Democratic majority placed further restrictions on the administration of unions. Meanwhile, some planters who were members of Congress received agricultural

[1] There is considerable difference in opinion among social scientists about the extent of change in values between 1929 and 1945. This seems inevitable because in the short-run values change unevenly based on age, status, and types of roles. The argument here is more directed to the well-substantiated fact that this period initiated changes in values, rather than to an effort, for which evidence is lacking, to assess the patterns in the new configuration.

benefit payments of as much as two to three hundred thousand dollars a year.

Thus, from 1945 on, in spite of liberal presidents and progressive legislative programmes, Congress blocked rather than stimulated social change.[1] The major liberal achievement of the period, more equal civil and political rights, was initiated by the Supreme Court in 1954, and only tardily and reluctantly supported by Congress over the ensuing decade. The personal influence of the Texan Lyndon B. Johnson on southern committee chairmen produced a mild progressive movement from 1963 to 1967, as illustrated by a stronger civil rights bill and medicare, but the pressures of the Vietnam War brought it to an early end.

The rapid rise of matériel and research expenditures for national defence from 1950 on created a second type of political bloc composed of the representatives of the very large prime contractors for military equipment and the men in government who decided where contracts were to be placed. Since government financed three-quarters of the mounting costs of new research and development, such grants were also a matter of continuous bargaining between big business and government departments. Needless to say, there was a considerable movement of experienced technicians between these two types of employers, and the trade unions involved in such production supported military expenditure.

Most of the many changes brought about by the Great Depression and the war became, rather unconsciously, parts of accepted American social learning and institutions. The most deeply disturbing change for both the political and business élite was the new situation in world affairs. The degree of what might well be termed 'cultural shock' can only be understood fully in the light of the unique international history of the United States. Since 1815 the people of the United States had never feared encroachment on their homeland by a foreign power. Generations

[1] Blocking specific legislative or deliberate change, of course, has often very little effect on actual rates of social change which result from the continuous process of roles and institutions altering to fit new technological, demographic, or other altered conditions.

enjoying both oceanic and Britannic security had had only a mild interest in what went on abroad. Before 1916 it is doubtful if a foreign issue had ever been of major importance in a presidential election.

When stirred to action at the end of the century by its own marketing possibilities and the quickened tempo of western world imperialism, the government had developed the 'Open Door Policy', an insistence on the right to trade in any area on equal terms with other foreign nations. At the same time the nation also joined in the imperial race, fought a prolonged colonial war, acquired various types of colonies, and marked out an exclusive investment area in Central America and the Caribbean. The old American sense of mission, of duty to the world, readily cloaked decisions, made by military force, in the mantle of inevitable and beneficent progress, and still did in 1970. Yet the whole group interested in foreign affairs was small, and their ideas and interests probably had little effect on domestic change. Americans did not see themselves as citizens of an aggressive power or as part of western world imperialism. And, in spite of colonial territories, up to the 1950s it was believed in high business circles that the nation need not assume more expense for foreign political controls because, given an equal chance, United States trade and finance could compete successfully anywhere in the world.

This concept of the power of the nation's business, often confused with isolationism, dominated Republican policy following World War I. It was thought by leaders of politics and business that the United States did not need membership in a League of Nations, or formal treaties of alliance; that the power of Wall Street finance could control the course of world events; and to a large degree it did until the crash of 1929. As in Germany, Italy and Japan, the depression replaced the representatives of business by men of military power, partly because of financial inaction by the American government (see the previous chapter), all types of leaders in the United States realized too late that their course had now deprived them of international influence. Many, particularly in Middle America, decided that the best solution was to withdraw from world affairs and build a national or western-hemisphere defence.

The result of World War II was to reverse the situation of the twenties and thirties: then the failure of the United States to take effective diplomatic or military action, and the exclusion of the Soviet Union, as far as possible, from entering into the system of balances, had created a vacuum. Germany and Austria had only been defeated by a concert of powers including the United States. Now England and France were left alone to police a European settlement highly unpopular in Germany, Italy and Russia. In 1945 there was no question that the United States and Russia, each representing overwhelming military force in relation to that of other nations, would play active parts in world affairs. But it was equally true that neither had foreign offices nor traditions of diplomacy suitable for world leadership. Because of its enormous economic power and sole possession of the atomic bomb, the United States was initially much the stronger, or more menacing as a 'bull in a china shop'. What to do with such power was a problem far beyond a President from Missouri, chiefly versed in domestic local politics, or a Secretary of State best known for creating a pleasing personal image. Since Roosevelt, also, was far from being a calculating student of international affairs, his death in April, 1945, may have made relatively little difference. The leaders of the United States, in general, were emotionally and intellectually unprepared for the roles in foreign affairs that were thrust upon them.

While the basic decision to build up West Germany and not to aid Russia would probably have had the support of most businessmen and voters, the educated American public knew little about the real issues in 1945 and 1946. Fed by the mass media, a fear of communism at home and Russian influence abroad swept over the United States, while suspicion that America wanted to undo some of the results of the war and check Russia by a rebuilt Germany scared the then exhausted and economically weak Soviet Union. With these mutual fears and the resulting unfriendly actions, no common ground for international dialogue was possible.

During the ensuing 'Cold War' no sufficiently persuasive leaders in the United States conceived of trade by businessmen as a long-run force that could gradually and peacefully undermine and subvert communism. Communist governments were feared as the type wanted by less-developed peoples—irrevocable, once established, and united by a common, world-wide bond— rather than as a phase of political change that was generating its own serious and possibly destructive problems. In other words, too many United States businessmen, in spite of themselves, were good Marxists thinking in terms of impending and lasting world revolution which could only be prevented by force, rather than men confidently trusting in the power of acquisitive desires and ultimate national resistance to end restraints on trade or overthrow unwanted political controls.[1] Both business and political leaders exhibited the historic American traits of impatience, a desire for action, and missionary moral certainties. To some degree the 3,500 United States military bases around the world and enormous expenditures for intelligence and equipment were efforts to re-establish the old feeling of security that had existed before World War I, but the normal institutional drives of such vast organizations for defence were to strive to magnify the problems that justified their existence.

In domestic politics the men who had the most familiarity with foreign affairs found it difficult, even if they tried, to change the emotional attitudes or values of the people in nine-tenths of the area of the United States. What in earlier years had been anti-semitism, anti-catholicism, or just dislike of foreigners in general, was now easily translated into fear of communism and distrust of international agencies. In small cities all over the country local businessmen saw the United Nations as a subversive force, many still wanted the withdrawn 'fortress America', argued for by their

---

[1] To gain force and exert leadership men in power are inclined to act as though they could predict history, but they seldom carefully check their conclusions with panels of historians, or, if they do, as in the case of John F. Kennedy, they only take the advice that seems best politically.

earlier champion Robert A. Taft, and meanwhile they thought it good to keep the army up to the mark by fighting communism.

As was seen in Chapter III, keeping the army at work, particularly in Southeast Asia, had unfortunate repercussions on youth in the United States, not only because the specific actions seemed inhumane, but because Asian policy, as a whole, appeared to have been stumbled into rather than carefully thought through. Furthermore, some journalists wrote that among all anti-war demonstrators there ran the conviction that the Vietnam War was 'an old man's war', caused by another generation's commitments.[1] The future problem was whether the great Asian powers—China, India, Japan, Pakistan and Russia—could not be allowed to work out their own destinies independently of the United States, or whether the latter was obliged, for its own safety, to assume the same balancing role that England had played for centuries in relation to continental Europe. That the United States was much stronger and further away than England had been seemed a strong argument in favour of at least trying benevolent neutrality.

This book started with the paradox that the United States was in 1900 perhaps the most advanced nation in the world technologically and backward in relation to the social ideas and attitudes then prevalent in Europe. By 1970 a different paradox had appeared; although the United States still led the world technologically and was in general abreast of the progress of western thought, its citizenry were unprepared for the world position that the nation's size and technological proficiency and the march of events had forced upon them. Institutions and the ideas of role-sets, on subjects which lay outside the range of everyday life, had changed only gradually while external events had moved more rapidly, making the perception and attitude of the average citizen, or the sanctions of his role-sets, regarding foreign affairs, largely unrealistic.

Such dysfunctionalism, added to that arising from other types

---

[1] Bruce Kublick, 'History as a Way of Learning', *American Quarterly* XXII (Autumn 1970), p. 621.

of social change, such as the cumulative pressures of population and new technology, or that initiated by new ideas in science and other fields of learning. The world of 1970 was simply too much, not only for the average citizen, but probably in all its ramifications beyond the grasp of anyone. While an assumption of the role scheme is that change is continuous and hence roles and institutions are always to some degree dysfunctional, the problems of readjustment vary in magnitude and in how much the new behaviour fits or conflicts with existing institutions. In the field of foreign affairs the conflict was understandably severe.

CHAPTER XI

CHARACTERISTICS OF TWENTIETH-CENTURY CHANGE

In reading the history of England, France, Germany or the United States in the twentieth century, the impression of sameness in problems and attempted solutions, if not in their timing, is far stronger than that of national uniqueness or any important superiorities. In all of these nations major social institutions underwent great changes in the relatively brief period of three-quarters of a century. Religion, morality, education, technology, community structure, social security and governmental participation in society were drastically altered, and in the same directions. In technology, natural resources, and scale of industrial operations the United States was a leader, and this carried with it an affluence that made some social problems less pressing. In addition, both fixed constitutions and controversial divisions of power within the American federal system often made action more difficult than in unified governments. Hence, in the use of the state to provide greater security of all kinds, to safeguard the rights of labour to organize, and to improve housing, the United States lagged behind the European leaders. Yet a generation later the United States usually adopted measures quite similar to those that had proved workable in Europe. Only the position of the millions of black men remained as a uniquely American problem.

Institutional change in the Western world has to be seen against a background of the weakening of the old, internalized sanctions based on earlier types of prestige, customs, and religious authority. Scientific psychological knowledge appeared to rob man of his will-power, and of belief that he was created in the image of God. On the one hand, it made all changes easier and, on the other, it made any results seem less rewarding. After the inner revolution no new justification for the institutions and internalized restraints necessary to hold society together appeared to be as satisfactory as an accepted hierarchical social structure and an authoritarian religion. Men in all the western nations sought in vain for an emotionally satisfying and socially justifiable 'escape from freedom'.

In contrast, in the world of technology, new methods and resulting freedoms gave new hope of solving many of the age-old material problems. Work routines in limited areas of manufacturing reached a maximum of unpleasantness early in the century, as factories grew bigger and assembly lines more demanding, but then took a turn for the better as service and trade grew in relation to industry, the small plant superseded the large, processes governed by valves and meters grew in importance, and more of the population worked for medium-sized employers. By 1970, knowledge rather than physical energy seemed the requirement of the future, and the old 'blue-collar' manual workers in industry destined to become a smaller group. Between 1945 and 1970 this process had already taken place in agriculture. The commercial farmer needed many kinds of scientific and mechanical knowledge, but only the physical energy necessary to guide machines.

New technology and processes had less effect on the majority who laboured in mining, transportation, trade, and service, but these workers had seldom experienced the more frustrating routines of minutely specialized operations, or the dawn-to-dusk physical demands of old-style farming. Even in these great areas where human operations were still necessary, the physical strains were eased by machines, no one carried hundred-pound cakes of ice or bags of coal, and very few cleaned stables or shod horses. Yet a demand for higher levels of knowledge in nearly all occupational roles might be a harder one for the next generation to meet than the physical demands of the past. No one knew how large a percentage of the population, given proper early training, could rise to a given level of expertness.

In many ways the individual, although dependent on the functioning of a vast amount of technology, had more apparent social choice than in earlier ages.[1] Families served by television were more self-sufficient from the standpoint of a variety of leisure-time entertainment than those on farms or even in most cities had been in earlier days. The automobile allowed movement in any direction for either work or recreation. By 1970 the spread of mobile homes in the United States was beginning to threaten the whole conception of long-term geographically fixed dwellings. Even though most American families had always moved about every five years, they could now accelerate the process without changing their house. This development was only in its earliest stages by 1970 and was, of course, resisted by the politically powerful construction industry. The long-run social effects of this and other geographical dimensions of freedom, including easy world-wide movement, were still not clear, but they made for a more uniform national and world culture.

The technological trend in electricity and motor vehicles that preserved the small businessman in manufacturing had political repercussions. In such enterprise as well as in most trade and service operations the old-style, profit-seeking capitalist survived. Still believing in self-help and resenting government interference, such men represented a powerful influence in state and local government and were directly represented by many of their own kind in Congress. In contrast, the chief executives of large corporate bureaucracies were coming to see the economically important social relations of their companies as both broad and long-term, and their relations with government as necessarily close and often financially helpful. There was, therefore, a growing rift in the attitudes of the business community between

[1] The view of Herbert Marcuse that these leisure-time activities were a means of sustaining 'surplus repression' by élite groups, and the possible influence of mass media were discussed in Chapters III and V.

relatively liberal or, at least, non-*laissez-faire* big company executives and extremely conservative smaller proprietors, with the rapidly growing number of the latter group likely to exert the most continuous political influence.

Regardless of the size of enterprise, economic developments ran contrary to certain social trends. From 1950 on, a smaller proportion of all workers was needed to manufacture consumer products. While military demand tended to arrest what might otherwise have been an absolute decline, the growing civilian need for labour and innovation in the economy was in all forms of service. Yet, except for finance and some special forms such as hotel management, service was not attractive to able, well-educated young men. College graduates preferred the professions, government or careers in big corporations. Few wanted to service the complicated new machinery that was so readily produced, or to perform functions that earlier generations had stamped as menial. Thus by the 1960s there was an imperfect adjustment of supply and demand in labour that produced, for example, a surplus of college teachers and shortage of men properly trained for repairing electrical equipment.

Building construction and maintenance, lying between factory work and service, was, in most urban areas, tightly organized on a union basis resembling the old craft guilds. But, as more and more units were prefabricated, and the federal government, in the middle 1960s, restricted housing by smaller grants and tighter money, construction went into a decline as an area of employment. The nation needed many buildings, however, and ultimately, in spite of more prefabrication, there might be an increase in the relative demand for such skilled and semi-skilled labour, which to most high-school graduates seem preferable to service.

The strong unions were in mining, manufacturing, transportation, and construction, with little representation in trade, service or finance. Therefore, during the period from 1953, the peak of Korean War activity, to 1970 there was a secular decline in the percentage of organized workers from 25 to more nearly 20 per cent of the labour force. Yet, in spite of this loss in over-all strength, because of the readiness of government and big business to avoid disruptive strikes by meeting wage demands, the unions were pace-setters in a steady 'wage push' inflation that became a major social and economic problem in all democratic societies. Since the 'push' went on in spite of rising unemployment, it illustrated an economic factor based on organized social power, and not explicable on the basis of conventional theory. Consequently, there was in 1970 widespread disagreement as to proper democratic remedies.

One of the most distinctive features of the United States throughout its history had been the continuous shifting of population. In the first decade of the century the continuing westward movement was more than equalled by a vast influx of eastern and southern European immigrants who settled primarily in the coastal and middle western industrial centres. When this foreign influex was checked by World War I and ensuing restriction of immigration, negroes and other impoverished farm workers were drawn to the cities in periods of high employment, leading to an ever larger metropolitan population. Since there are fundamental differences between the face-to-face role-sets and personally given sanctions of rural areas and the more remote impersonal relations of cities, in their effects on character and role-playing, the decline in agricultural households from a third of the total in 1900 to about one-twentieth in 1970 was one of the most significant social changes in the twentieth century.

But the change in personality and behaviour was more complex than a mere rural urban contrast. From World War II on, the movement of both business and people from central city to suburban fringe areas, accelerating into an 'urban explosion', was accompanied by important changes which produced a domestic 'third world'. The role-set and sanctions of the suburban community had some of the reinforcing face-to-face character of the country, yet there were differences that made adjustment, for many, more difficult than in the city. The role-sets shifted frequently, friendships were shallow, a high degree of conformity was expected in community attitudes, and the economic status ladder was starkly visible.

On the economic side, shifts in population also produced changes that laid the basis for new ways of life. Packaged (equal monthly payments), long-term mortgages, guaranteed for most families by the government, produced a rise in home-ownership from 44 per cent of all household units in 1940 to about 70 per cent thirty years later. The needs of suburbanites for easy parking and the possibility of lower prices from large-scale retail distribution led to the movement of shopping centres away from the old built-up market towns. In some instances new small cities on the urban fringe grew up around major highway intersections and varied shopping facilities, forecasting a new type of spread-out, but not necessarily planned, industrial centre.

During all of the period before 1940 there was no adequate planning either for the housing of the millions of new urbanites, or for the proper business expansion of cities. The long-intrenched traditions of *laissez-faire* and limited government, in general, made city planning difficult. Furthermore, in the years after World War II some earlier ideas of planning proved undesirable. The high-rise, government-subsidized apartment building, widely used in Europe, turned out to be unsatisfactory in much of the United States. Demolition of old-time slums and replacement by high-rise structures destroyed the community life of the streets, increased crime, and usually failed to rehouse the same people who had been forced to vacate. The idea of the separation of manufacturing, trade, and residential areas, one of the major tenets of early planning, also conflicted with that of neighbourhood urban communities. In the future the attractive shop and clean factory might open the way to different solutions.

Insurance and other companies with large reserves began in the 1960s to build some completely new moderate-sized cities as had the government in Great Britain. In all, the distribution of population was still changing rapidly in the 1970s, and none of the minor moves in the direction of planning had proved altogether satisfactory.

How to build and where to live were only part of the array of problems that challenged the United States more than at any time in its history. Foreign affairs in the 1960s were highly unsatisfactory because of a large-scale and continuing foreign war, but, aside from this immediate trouble, no satisfactory long-run adjustments had been made between the major military powers. Partly this was because, in addition to all the age-old problems of balance of power, the United States had a deep fear of communism which was shared in reverse by a fear of expanding capitalism in China, Russia, and many smaller powers.

It could be hoped that explosively dangerous foreign relations, while raising the possibility of human destruction, were a passing problem. More disturbing, if society survived at all, were unprecedented rates of internal social change. Not only did the increasingly rapid trend toward a literally inconceivable computerized society relegate much social or economic theory to a lost world of the past, but new distributions of power or authority caused by institutional changes threatened to create increasingly severe social tensions. One of these, of great importance in 1970, was between the groups that could keep abreast with or gain from the steady inflation that resulted from the strength of labour in wage bargaining and the high costs of the welfare state, and those who feared both for themselves and for the future of capitalism. Since the latter group included the holders of stocks, bonds, and pensions, backed by the organized financial interests, they had the power to take strong and possibly undemocratic action. Another series of crises would come as automation forced unionized workers and many of their managers out of industry and into new services.

Other tensions involved the problems of democracy in time-honoured social institutions. In the leading western nations government had been democratized in the nineteenth century, but the hierarchical institutions of agrarian aristocracy in learning, the relation of the sexes, the family, the arts, and the church, together with the authoritarian relations of proprietary business, had come into the twentieth century largely unchanged. By 1960 the spread of advanced knowledge and the decline of manual effort required by the new technology added to the rebelliousness of youth in general, and women in particular, against these authoritarian institutions of the past. The resulting conflicts of the mid-century over giving students and teachers more control of education, over broader opportunities for women, over moving control of the arts from wealthy patrons to larger, younger groups, over democratizing church government, and over replacing dictatorial paternalism by more consultative, bargaining types of management in business could be seen as later stages in the movement against hierarchical orders earlier manifest in the American and French revolutions.

In spite of the pessimism of some deductive philosophers, it seemed at least possible that coming generations might progress toward psychic 'liberation' through the advance of the democratic as against the hierarchical principle and faith in the future of man. Each of the industrial nations differed somewhat as to the parts of their society where hierarchical principles had been most weakened. In the United States, for example, democracy had made considerable advances in the arts, education, and religion, but far less in business and military affairs. In some other nations the military was not very important and business had moved further toward participatory democracy by employees, while education and religion still remained authoritarian. Even in the big American corporation the increasing reliance on computers might limit and define the possible options to a point where democratic decision, as by a representative council, would be as effective as authoritarian control by one man. In a highly educated society the conflicts of the more distant future might be over the proper size of units for making decisions in different spheres of activity rather than over the principle of non-hierarchical democratic control.

ADDITIONAL READING

Since few historians or other social scientists have written specifically on the nature of social change in major institutions, it is hard to select revelant reading. In general, books are suggested that will supply background material for the generalizations made in the indicated chapter.

CHAPTER I: *A Systematic Approach to Change*
The two most comprehensive volumes on the concepts used in the role paradigm are Bruce J. Biddle and Edwin J. Thomas, ed., *Role Theory: Concepts and Research* (New York and Chichester, Sussex: John Wiley, 1966), and Amitai and Eva Etzioni, eds., *Social Change: Sources, Patterns and Consequences* (New York: Basic Books, 1964). Wilbert E. Moore's *Social Change* (Englewood Cliffs, N.J., and Hemel Hempstead, Herts: Prentice Hall, 1964) is a briefer, readable synthesis. Warner J. Cahnman and Alvin Boskoff, eds., *Sociology and History: Theory and Research* (New York: Free Press, 1964, and London: Collier-Macmillan, 1964) has articles on many of the areas of interest for one studyng social change.

CHAPTER II: *The Inner Revolution*
A general view of intellectual trends can be gained from Merle E. Curti, *The Growth of American Thought* (New York and London: Harper & Row, 3rd edn., 1964). Thought of the first two decades of the century is well summarized in Henry F. May, *The End of American Innocence** (New York: Knopf, 1959). William James, *Pragmatism, A New Name for Old Ways of Thinking* (New York: Longmans Green, 1916, and many other editions from 1907 on) is highly readable and representative of the new attitudes. Another contemporary view is Jane Addams, *Democracy and Social Ethics* (Cambridge, Mass.: Belknap Press of Harvard University Press, 1964). See also: Erich Fromm, *Psychoanalysis and Religion** (New Haven and London: Yale University Press, 1958; Philip Rieff, *Freud: The Mind of a Moralist** (New York: Viking, 1959, London: Gollancz, 1960); Sir James Jeans, *The Mysterious Universe** (New York: Macmillan, 1930, 2nd edn., Cambridge: Cambridge University Press, 1948); and Albert N. Whitehead, *Science in the Modern World** (New York: Macmillan, 1926; Cambridge: Cambridge University Press, 1946).

CHAPTER III: *The Search for Justification*
The theme of the chapter is so broad that the literature seems limitless. On what was happening in the churches see: Charles H. Hopkins, *The Rise of the Social Gospel in American Prostestantism, 1865-1915* (New Haven and London: Yale University Press, 1940); Robert M. Miller, *American Protestantism and Social Issues, 1919-1937* (Chapel Hill: University of North Carolina Press, 1958); Will Herberg, *Protestant, Catholic and Jew** (Garden City: Doubleday, 1955); and *Daedalus, Religion in America* (Boston: Winter, 1967). Reinhard

* Indicates availability in a paperback edition.

Bendix's *Work and Authority in Industry: Ideologies of Management in the Course of Industrialization* (New York: Wiley, 1956, London: Harper & Row) has a long chapter on twentieth-century United States. On philosophies that have appealed to the younger generations see: Mary Warnock, *Existentialism** (Oxford: Oxford University Press, 1970); Alasdair MacIntyre, *Marcuse** (London: Collins, 1970); Herbert Marcuse, *Eros and Civilization** (Boston: Beacon Press, 1955, London: Sphere Books, 1969).

CHAPTER IV: *Education and Democracy*
Books on the history of education that consider its relation to general social change and also cover the 1960s are lacking. Among earlier studies see: Isaac L. Kandell, *American Education in the Twentieth Century* (Cambridge, Mass: Harvard University Press, 1957), and William C. De Vane, *Higher Education in Twentieth Century America* (Cambridge, Mass.: Harvard University Press, 1965). Laurence A. Cremin, *Transformation of the School: Progressivism in American Education, 1876–1957*) (New York: Knopf, 1961) is a well-written account of the movement for 'progressive education'. See also: Andre Daniere, *Higher Education in the American Economy** (New York: Random House, 1964).

CHAPTER V: *Communication and Community*
The problem of creating a sense of community in urban mass society is discussed in essays on *The Search for Community in Modern America,** edited by E. Digby Baltzell (New York: Harper & Row, 1968). Two penetrating discussions of advertising are: Otis Pease, *The Responsibility of American Advertising: Private Control and Public Influence* (New Haven: Yale University Press, 1958), and David M. Potter, *People of Plenty** (Chicago: University of Chicago Press, 1954). Lewis Jacobs, *Rise of the American Film* (New York: Teachers College, Columbia University, 1939), covers the period of expansion. Erik Barnouw's three volumes under the series title *The Golden Web: A History of Broadcasting in the United States* (New York: Oxford University Press, 1971) are detailed but popularized. On the theoretical problems of communication see Melvin E. De Fleur, *Theories of Mass Communication** (2nd edn., New York: McKay, 1970), and for some extreme views Marshall McLuhan, *Understanding Media** (London: Routledge, 1964, Sphere Books, 1967).

CHAPTER VI: *The Dual Revolution*
My own *American Business System 1900–1955** (Cambridge, Mass.: Harvard University Press, 1957, London: Harper & Row), gives a general picture of twentieth-century technological and business change. There is no comprehensive volume on the diverse effects of electricity, but a recent book on the computer is Roger Meetham *Information Retrieval: The Essential Technology* (London: Aldus Books, 1969). On the automobile, James J. Flink, *America Adopts the Automobile, 1895-1910* (Cambridge, Mass.: M.I.T. Press, 1970) is broad social history. Allan Nevins and Frank E. Hill, *Ford*, 3 vols. (New York: Scribner, 1954–63) is a thorough treatment of both Henry Ford and the company. On the

* Indicates availability in a paperback edition.

industry as a whole see: Alfred D. Chandler, Jr., *Giant Enterprise: Ford, General Motors and the Automobile Industry* (New York: Harcourt, Brace, 1964) and John B. Rae, *The American Automobile: A Brief History** (Chicago: Chicago University Press, 1967).

CHAPTER VII: *Proprietary and Managerial Enterprise*

There is no general history of the modal types of American business. Economists and historians have both been fascinated by the rise of a small number of giant companies, and on these the literature is voluminous. Alfred D. Chandler, Jr., *Strategy and Structure: Chapters in the History of American Industrial Enterprise** (Cambridge, Mass.: Harvard University Press, 1962) is a good account of the evolution of managerial practice in four big firms. Wilbert E. Moore, in *The Conduct of the Corporation: A Spirited Invasion of the Privacy of the Big Companies** (New York: Vintage, 1962), writes from a sociological view. Samuel Haber in *Efficiency and Uplift: Scientific Management in the Progressive Era 1890–1920* (Chicago and London: Chicago University Press, 1964) sets early management thought in its social context. Francis X. Sutton and others, *The American Business Creed* (Cambridge, Mass.: Harvard University Press, 1956, London: Bailey Bros., 1956) deals with the mid-twentieth-century ideas and attitudes of businessmen. William H. Whyte, Jr.'s *The Organization Man** (London: Penguin) is a broad view of the big corporation's social influence, as is C. Wright Mills's *The Power Elite* (New York: Oxford University Press, 1957). Both books contain some exaggerations.

CHAPTER VIII: *Demographic Forces*

Two good books on immigration are Oscar Handlin, ed., *Immigration as a Factor in American History** (Englewood Cliffs, N.J.: Prentice-Hall, 1959), and John Higham, *Strangers in the Land** (New York: Atheneum, 1963); Richard A. Easterlin in *Population, Labor Force and Long Swings in Economic Growth: The American Experience* (Princeton: National Bureau of Economic Research, 1968) makes illuminating applications of demographic data. Study of the city as the major location of contemporary society has attracted few historians, in contrast to much writing by economists and 'urbanologists'. Blake McKelvey's *The Emergence of Metropolitan America 1915–1966* (New Brunswick: Rutgers University Press, 1968) is the most comprehensive history.

CHAPTER IX: *From Family to Institutional Security*

This chapter and the next are chiefly centred on the period of the New Deal. My own *The Great Depression and World War II** (Glenview, Ill.: Scott, Foresman, 1967) gives a general and partly theoretical view. The slowness of private assumption of the security burden is discussed in John R. Commons and others, *History of Labor in the United States,* Vol. III (New York: Macmillan, 1935). Because of the worldwide influence of the British economist on stability and social security, it is worth reading a monograph such as Robert Lekachman, *The Age of Keynes** (London: Alan Lane, 1967).

* Indicates availability in a paperback edition.

ADDITIONAL READING

CHAPTER X: *Disruptive Change*

For an economic interpretation of foreign policy and wars see William A. Williams, *The Tragedy of American Diplomacy** (New York: Dell, 1959). Foreign policy after 1945 is treated in a mildly revisionist way in Walter La Febers' *America, Russia and the Cold War 1945–1966* (New York: Wiley, 1967) and in a strongly revisionist manner, with emphasis on Vietnam, in Gabriel Kolko, *The Roots of American Foreign Policy** (Boston: Beacon Press, 1969).

For the profound effect of depression on the labour movement see two comprehensive volumes by Irvin Bernstein, *The Lean Years 1920–1933: A History of the American Worker* (Boston: Houghton Mifflin, 1960), and *The Turbulent Years 1933–1941: A History of the American Worker* (Boston: Houghton Mifflin, 1970). Sidney Fine's *Sit Down: The General Motors Strike of 1936–1937* (Ann Arbor: University of Michigan Press, 1969) places a single labour action in a broad historical and social setting. Alan K. McAdams, *Power and Politics in Labor Legislation* (New York: Columbia University Press, 1964) covers the last major Congressional action and illustrates the pressures affecting labour legislation.

* Indicates availability in a paperback edition

INDEX

72 73 74 75   12 11 10 9 8 7 6 5 4 3 2 1